WRITTEN IN STONE

ENGLISH HERITAGE

WRITTEN IN STONE

JILL SHARP

Published by English Heritage, 23 Savile Row, London W1S 2ET

Copyright © English Heritage 2005
First published March 2005
The author's moral rights are asserted.

Product code 51009
ISBN 1 85074 9299

A CIP catalogue for this book is available from the British Library.

English Heritage is the Government's statutory adviser on archaeology,
conservation and the management of the historic environment in England. English
Heritage provides expert advice to the Government about all matters relating to
the historic environment and its conservation.

A number of the sites in this book are in the guardianship of English
Heritage but managed by other organisations. For management details, as
well as locations, entry times and prices, please refer to our website:
www.english-heritage.org.uk

Edited by Julia Elliott
Designed by Rod Teasdale, White Rabbit Editions
Index by Sue Vaughan
Printed by Bath Press

HALF-TITLE PAGE: carved corbel at Furness Abbey, with (from top) Wordsworth, Jon Silkin and the Brontë sisters.

TITLE PAGE: Framlingham Castle, with (from top) Thomas Hardy, the Venerable Bede and John Cowper Powys.

Contents

Acknowledgements

Thanks are due to the following people within English Heritage who made suggestions for the book: Jeremy Ashbee, David Bailey, Nick Balaam, Nicola Bexon, Judy Brewis, David Brock, Julius Bryant, Gill Campbell, Caroline Carr-Whitworth, Jonathan Coad, Michael Constantine, Louise Dando, Keith Emerick, Charlotte Foster, Kath Graham, Andy Hammon, Val Horsler, Edward Impey, Hugh Jones, Zoe King, Jonathan Last, David Myles, Alastair Oswald, Ian Oxley, Rob Parkes, Caroline Pegum, Georgina Plowright, Ricky Pound, Giles Proctor, David Sherlock, Ann Todd, Susie West, Rebecca Wilson, Margaret Wood, and Chris Young. The help of Henry Vivian-Neal at Kensal Green Cemetery was particularly appreciated. Special thanks to Stephen Wainman for comment on the draft, to Rod Teasdale for the design and to my editor, Julia Elliott.

Credits

Extracts from the following works are reproduced by kind permission of the author, publisher or other copyright holder as indicated: Peter Ackroyd, *Hawksmoor* (Hamish Hamilton); W H Auden, *Collected Poems* (Faber and Faber); John Cowper Powys, *Maiden Castle* (Simon and Schuster); A E Housman, *Collected Poems* (Society of Authors); Rudyard Kipling, *Puck of Pook's Hill* (A P Watt); Andrew Motion, *Salt Water* (Faber and Faber); Gwen Raverat, *Period Piece* (Faber and Faber); Jon Silkin, *Collected Poems* (the Literary Estate of Jon Silkin); Rosemary Sutcliff, *The Eagle of the Ninth* (Oxford University Press) copyright © Anthony Lawton 1954.

English Heritage photographs taken by: Jonathan Bailey, Alun Bull, Steve Cole, Nigel Corrie, James Davies, Paul Highnam, Mike Kipling, Pat Payne, Graeme Peacock, Jeremy Richards, Bob Skingle, Andrew Tryner, and Peter Williams. All images are either © English Heritage or © Crown Copyright NMR unless otherwise stated as follows (page numbers in italics):

Mary Evans Picture Library: Thomas Hardy *2*; John Cowper Powys *13*; the Venerable Bede *52*; Gertrude Bell *56*; Discretion, Prudence, etc. *91*.

National Portrait Gallery, London: William Wordsworth *40*; W H Auden *44*; The Brontë Sisters *66*; Jon Silkin *68* (© Ruth Dupré/NPG); Richard III *71*; Sir Walter Scott *76*; Andrew Motion *81*(© Steven Speller/NPG); Samuel Pepys *83*; Alfred, 1st Baron Tennyson *95*; Charles Darwin *110*; Jane Austen *126*; Henry Wriothesley *129*.

Skyscan Balloon Photography: Old Sarum *6*, Maiden Castle *12*, Launceston Castle *14*, Pevensey Castle *122*.

Every effort has been made to trace copyright holders and we apologise in advance for any unintentional omissions, which we would be pleased to correct in any subsequent edition of the book.

The Writers

Peter Ackroyd	*born* 1949	W H Hudson		1841–1922
Aelred of Rievaulx	*c* 1110–1167	Thomas Hughes		1822–1896
Matthew Arnold	1822–1888	Leigh Hunt		1784–1859
W H Auden	1907–1973	John Keats		1795–1821
Jane Austen	1775–1817	Margery Kempe	*c* 1373–*c*1440
Reverend Richard Barham	1788–1845	Francis Kilvert		1840–1879
The Venerable Bede	673–735	Rudyard Kipling		1865–1936
Gertrude Bell	1868–1926	John Leland	*c* 1506–1552
William Bowles	1762–1850	Nicholas Love	*died c* 1423
Anne Brontë	1820–1849	John Lydgate	*c* 1370–*c*1449
Charlotte Brontë	1816–1855	Sir Thomas Malory	*died* 1471
John Bunyan	1628–1688	Henry Mayhew		1812–1887
Samuel Butler	1613–1680	Richard Methley	*c* 1450–*c*1527
Samuel Butler	1835–1902	Andrew Motion	*born* 1952
Caedmon	*fl* 670	Samuel Pepys		1633–1703
Geoffrey Chaucer	*c* 1343–1400	Alexander Pope		1688–1744
G K Chesterton	1874–1936	John Cowper Powys		1872–1963
William Cobbett	1763–1835	Sir Walter Raleigh		1552–1618
Samuel Taylor Coleridge	1772–1834	Ralph of Coggeshall	*fl* 1207–1226
Wilkie Collins	1824–1889	Terence Rattigan		1911–1979
Thomas Creevey	1768–1838	Gwen Raverat		1885–1957
Charles Darwin	1809–1882	Sir Walter Scott		1771–1832
Daniel Defoe	1660–1731	William Shakespeare		1564–1616
Charles Dickens	1812–1870	Jon Silkin		1930–1997
Arthur Conan Doyle	1859–1930	William Sotheby		1757–1833
Ebenezer Elliott	1781–1849	Laurence Sterne		1713–1768
John Evelyn	1620–1706	Bram Stoker		1847–1912
John Meade Falkner	1858–1932	Rosemary Sutcliff		1920–1992
Celia Fiennes	1662–1741	Jonathan Swift		1667–1745
George Fox	1624–1691	Algernon Charles Swinburne		1837–1909
Elizabeth Gaskell	1810–1865	Alfred, Lord Tennyson		1809–1892
John Gay	1685–1732	William Makepeace Thackeray		1811–1863
Geoffrey of Monmouth	*died* 1155	Anthony Trollope		1815–1882
Thomas Gray	1716–1771	Virgil		70–19BC
Bishop Guy of Amiens	1058–1075	Horace Walpole		1717–1797
Thomas Hardy	1840–1928	Izaak Walton		1593–1683
Thomas Hobbes	1588–1679	Richard Warner		1763–1857
Mary Hogarth	1819–1837	T H White		1906–1964
A E Housman	1859–1936	Lady Jane Wilde	*c* 1821–1896
Henry Howard	*c* 1517–1547	William Wordsworth		1770 1850

Foreword

Peveril Castle

England is not only a land defined by cartographers, or the location of a political and cultural identity; it is also a landscape of the imagination. The traveller who reads is accompanied on the road by a host of writers past and present, and by the characters they have created. When we arrive at Whitby Bram Stoker and Dracula are there before us; at Stonehenge we meet Hardy and Tess; and a veritable round table of historians, poets and novelists awaits the visitor to Tintagel.

Written in Stone takes a journey round England, visiting a selection of English Heritage sites that are linked to the writers whose works have shaped England's literary heritage. The historical significance of these sites varies, but each is unique. Some have been the birthplace or home of writers, or places they have visited at significant moments in their creative lives. Others have provided an atmosphere or a setting for a literary work, and some, like Powys's Maiden Castle, have even become characters themselves.

Certain prolific authors – Scott and Hardy, Wordsworth and Cobbett – are met frequently on the path; others, such as Chaucer and Jane Austen, are met in passing. Many works of outstanding repute are linked to these sites: Shakespeare's plays and sonnets, Romantic lyric poems and some of the great realist novels; but lesser-known books are also featured: Kilvert's *Diaries*, the *Journeys* of Celia Fiennes and the political papers of Thomas Creevey. Some of the texts brought to light along the way, like Lydgate's poetry and the novels of John Cowper Powys, would now be regarded by many as literary curiosities, but the traveller is also able to retrieve from behind the bookshelves some wonderful almost-forgotten texts: Falkner's

thrilling *Moonfleet*, Hardy's extraordinary play *The Dynasts* and Richard Barham's entertaining *Ingoldsby Legends*. Whatever their current status and reputation, all of these works have shaped and influenced the literary heritage we now enjoy.

As well as leading the reader from place to place, *Written in Stone* is a voyage in time, tracing the country's literature from its earliest poets and historians – Caedmon and Bede – through the medieval and early modern periods, the Romantics and Victorians, to the first poet laureate of the 21st century. In doing so it covers a remarkable diversity of genres – not only novels, drama and poetry, but also memoirs, diaries and travelogues, letters and gossip, science and politics, history, religion and philosophy.

The journey followed by *Written in Stone* is not exhaustive. Many writers have been drawn

to Stonehenge, for example, but not all of them have managed to conjure the excitement of Hardy's and Ackroyd's novels, or to describe with the perception of Hudson and Kilvert. Nor is it exhausting; the journey may be followed from beginning to end, but it is also easy for the reader to visit individual sites or explore them region by region.

En route will be met the great names and titles of English literature; but perhaps the greater pleasure will be in encountering the many lesser-known writers and works that still have the power to surprise. Their words, and the sites that have inspired them, tell some of the most absorbing stories in this volume.

The journey begins at Stonehenge and follows a broad sweep clockwise around England. The sequence and grouping of the sites within the book reflect the movements of the writers who visited them.

Stonehenge

England's foremost poet of the landscape, William Wordsworth, visited Stonehenge during a walking tour in 1793, passing across Salisbury Plain en route from the Isle of Wight to north Wales. It seems that the presence of the stones inspired visions of the ancient Britons that paradoxically restored for a time the poet's ever-wavering faith. He invokes the monument in grand style in *Guilt and Sorrow*; or *Incidents upon Salisbury Plain:*

> Pile of Stone-henge! so proud to hint yet keep
> Thy secrets, thou that lov'st to stand and hear
> The Plain resounding to the whirlwind's sweep,
> Inmate of lonesome nature's endless year ...
> Within that fabric of mysterious form
> Winds met in conflict, each by turns supreme.

The cleric and diarist Francis Kilvert was interested to learn, on meeting Wordsworth's niece, that the great poet 'could not bear the act of writing', when for him it was such a pleasure. Kilvert's diary, which covered the last nine years of his life, minutely records the landscape of

LEFT AND ABOVE **The ancient stone circle at Stonehenge. These great stones are the remnants of the last in a series of monuments erected on this site between about 3000 and 1600 BC.**

Wiltshire and rural life in mid-Victorian England. (It is also remarkably self-revealing, notably of the Reverend's absorption in the physical charms of very young women. Kilvert died suddenly from peritonitis only five weeks after his marriage, and his wife destroyed all but three of his twenty-two notebooks.) Kilvert described his first visit to Stonehenge in an entry for 27 August 1875. He is clearly awed by the place:

> Soon after we left the Druid's Head and struck across the turf eastward we came in sight of the grey cluster of gigantic Stones. They stood in the midst of a green plain, and the first impression they left on my mind was that of a group of people standing about and talking together. It seemed to me as if they were ancient giants who suddenly became silent and stiffened into stone directly anyone approached, but who might at any moment become alive again ... It is a solemn awful place. As I entered the charmed circle of the sombre Stones I instinctively uncovered my head. It was like entering a great Cathedral Church.

Thomas Hardy,
photograph by Alvin Langdon Coburn
(reproduced in Century *magazine).*

It was the winds that play through the stones, as well as its pagan associations, that made Stonehenge an ideal location for Thomas Hardy to use at the climax of his novel *Tess of the D'Urbervilles* (1891). At the beginning of the novel Tess, the innocent village lass, joins the other village girls in a springtide fertility dance, before setting out to fulfil her drunken father's wish and establish an ancestral connection between their family and the aristocratic D'Urbervilles. She is seduced and abandoned by Alec D'Urberville, and the child she bears soon dies. Working as a dairymaid, she then meets and falls in love with Angel Clare, but when she confesses her affair with D'Urberville on her wedding night, Angel abandons her.

Returning to her family, Tess by chance meets Alec, now a preacher, again, and reluctantly resumes her relationship with him. When Angel returns, Tess, desperate not to lose him a second time, stabs Alec. Tess and Angel wander through the New Forest for a few happy days before they are discovered and flee, exhausted, towards Salisbury Plain:

> They had proceeded thus gropingly two or three miles when on a sudden Clare became conscious of some vast erection close in his front, rising sheer from the grass. They had almost struck themselves against it.
> 'What monstrous place is this?' said Angel.
> 'It hums,' said she. 'Hearken!'
> He listened. The wind, playing upon the edifice, produced a

booming note of some gigantic one-stringed harp. No other sound came from it, and lifting his hand and advancing a step or two, Clare felt the vertical surface of the wall. It seemed to be of solid stone, without joint or moulding. Carrying his fingers onward he found that what he had come in contact with was a colossal rectangular pillar; by stretching out his left hand he could feel a similar one adjoining. At an indefinite height overhead something made the black sky blacker, which had the semblance of a vast architrave uniting the pillars horizontally. They carefully entered beneath and between; the surfaces echoed their soft rustle; but they seemed to be still out of doors. The place was roofless. Tess drew her breath fearfully, and Angel, perplexed, said –

'What can it be?'

Feeling sideways they encountered another tower-like pillar, square and uncompromising as the first; beyond it another and another. The place was all doors and pillars, some connected above by continuous architraves.

'A very Temple of the Winds,' he said.

The next pillar was isolated; others composed a trilithon; others were prostrate, their flanks forming a causeway wide enough for a carriage; and it was soon obvious that they made up a forest of monoliths grouped upon the grassy expanse of the plain. The couple advanced farther into this pavilion of the night till they stood in its midst.

'It is Stonehenge,' said Clare.

ABOVE View of the stones from inside the circle.

The detail of this description certainly benefits from Hardy's long training as an architect both in Dorchester and London, before he decided, with the support of Emma Gifford, his future wife, to earn a living from writing. The publication of *Tess* in 1891 caused a scandal because of its supposedly advanced views on sexual conduct – a scandal that naturally enhanced Hardy's reputation as a novelist.

But not all visitors have been instantly impressed by the site; of his first visit to these 'few old stones', traveller and naturalist W H Hudson wrote: 'It was one of the greatest disillusionments I ever experienced. Stonehenge was small – pitiably small!' Hudson was a great rambler, preferring to travel on foot and without a guidebook. He liked to experience the 'shock of pleasure' that comes from discovering a sight by chance so that, like Wordsworth before him, these experiences could became 'a permanent possession of the mind'.

It was on a subsequent visit that Hudson was to have his emotional experience, as he records in his *Afoot in England* (1909):

> Those rudely fashioned immemorial stones standing dark
> and large against the pale clear moonlit sky imparted
> something to the feeling. I sat among them alone and
> had them all to myself, as the others, fearing to tear their
> clothes on the barbed wire, had not ventured to follow
> me when I got through the fence.

Hudson had been born to American parents living in Argentina, but settled in England in 1869. His earlier books were studies on birds, but it was his writing on the English countryside that made his name, and influenced the back-to-nature movement of the 1920s and 1930s.

According to the novel *Hawksmoor* (1986) by Peter Ackroyd, Thomas Hardy had not been the only architect to appreciate the unique structural qualities of Stonehenge. Ackroyd's book weaves together the stories of Nicholas Dyer, apprentice to Sir Christopher Wren, who is commissioned to rebuild the London churches after the Great Fire, and modern-day detective Nicholas Hawksmoor, who is investigating a series of murders in the vicinity of these churches. Hawksmoor's solving of the murder mystery and Dyer's architectural plans unfold alternately, with Dyer's narrative including a visit with Sir Chris to Stonehenge:

He stopped to tye his Shooe, so then I flew ahead of him and first reached the Circle which was the Place of Sacrifice. And I bowed down.

Master Jones says it is erected on the Cubit measure, *says Sir Chris*. coming after me and taking out his Pocket-Book, and do you see, Nick, its beautiful Proportions?

It is a huge and monstrous Work, *I answered* standing straight, and it has been called the Architecture of the Devil.

But he paid no heed to me: They must have used tall trees for Levers, *he continu'd* squinting up at the Stones, or they discover'd the art of ordering Engines for the raising of Weights.

Some said Merlyn was the Father, *I replied*, and raised these Stones by the hidden Mysteries of Magick.

Sir Chris. laughed at this and sat upon the Stone in the inner Circle. There is an old rhyme, Nick, *says he*, which goes thus:

This Fame saies, Merlyn to perfection brought
But Fame said more than ever Merlyn wrought.

And he lean'd forward with a smile.

You are sitting on the Altar Stone, *I said*; and he jumped up quickly like one bitten. Do you see, *I continu'd*, how it is of a harder Stone and designed to resist Fire?

I see no Scorch marks, *he replied* ...

While Dyer continues to marvel at the mystic qualities of the place, Sir Chris examines the geometry of the stones, noting the 'Exactness of Placing them in regard to the Heavens'. But after sheltering from a rainstorm beneath one of the lintels, Sir Chris looks 'disconsolate to a strange Degree'. The great architect has succumbed to the power of the stones, and reveals to Dyer the contents of a disturbing vision.

Poets were writing about Stonehenge long before Wordsworth's late-18th-century verses, and it seems likely that Ackroyd's late-20th-century novel will not be the final literary visit to this unique site.

Old Sarum

It was William I's fear of invasion by the Danes that prompted him to commission the nationwide survey that was to become the *Domesday Book*. He needed to provision an army and raise the money to pay for it, so a detailed catalogue of land ownership, tax liability and military service provided an essential information bank.

Commissioned by William in December 1085, the survey took place over the following eight months, about 62,000 witnesses providing evidence on over 13,000 places in England and parts of Wales. 'Domesday Book' was a nickname given to the enterprise by the native English, comparing it to God's judgement day when all souls would be called to account, and the name was adopted by the official custodians of the two huge books in which the information was recorded. According to the anonymous scribe of the *Anglo-Saxon Chronicle:*

LEFT **Old Sarum:** an Iron Age hillfort constructed in about 500 BC and subsequently home to a castle, a palace and Salisbury's first cathedral.

> So very narrowly did he have it investigated that
> there was no single virgate of land, nor indeed (it is a
> shame to relate but it seemed no shame to him to
> do) one ox nor one cow nor one pig which there was
> left out, and not put down in his record; and all
> those records were brought to him afterwards ...

When the information was collected, William called a great convocation of his councillors at Old Sarum, so that he could formally receive the books, as well as their oaths of allegiance. The event is recorded in the *Anglo-Saxon Chronicle*:

> Then he travelled about so as to come to Salisbury at
> Lammas; and there his councillors came to him, and
> all the people occupying land who were of any
> account over England, no matter whose vassals they
> might be; and they all submitted to him and became
> his vassals and swore oaths of allegiance to him, that
> they would be loyal to him against all other men.

England's earliest public document, the *Domesday Book* is still valid as legal evidence of title to land, and it established at the start of the second millennium the pre-eminence of the centralised written record.

Sherborne Old Castle and Sherborne Castle

RIGHT **Ornamental details at Sherborne Old Castle: this 12th-century fortress was given by Elizabeth I to Sir Walter Raleigh.**

Adventurer, explorer and poet Sir Walter Raleigh was given
Sherborne Old Castle and its estate by Elizabeth I in 1592. His star was
briefly in the ascendant during the queen's displeasure with her
favourite, Essex, over his recent marriage. But when Elizabeth heard
that Raleigh had secretly wed Elizabeth Throckmorton, one of her
maids of honour, she imprisoned him in the Tower of London. Four
years earlier, in his poem *Farewell, false love*, Raleigh had contemplated
the nature of love in images that are far from idyllic:

> A maze wherein affection finds no end,
> A ranging cloud that runs before the wind,
> A substance like the shadow of the sun,
> A goal of grief for which the wisest run.

The queen released Raleigh after a few months and in 1595 he
embarked on an expedition to discover the fabled city of El Dorado,
returning from his journey along the Orinoco river in Guiana with
samples of gold. Although his wit and derring-do enabled him to survive
Elizabeth's reign he finally met an untimely death under James I. From
1603 to 1616 he was imprisoned in the Tower, along with his entire
family, on a charge of treason, finally being released because he insisted
he could bring back gold from a mine he had previously discovered in
Guiana. But the expedition resulted in the death of his eldest son, and
Raleigh returned without gold. He was executed in October 1618.

Raleigh became associated with a poetic group, known as the 'School
of Night', which was notorious for its political and religious scepticism,
and his poem *The Lie*, written while he was in prison, expresses attitudes
to those in power that still resonate in the 21st century:

> Tell Potentates they live   Tell men of high condition,
> Acting by others action,   That manage the estate,
> Not loved unless they give,   Their purpose is ambition,
> Not strong but by affection ...   Their practise only hate ...

Raleigh went to some trouble to modernise the 12th-century fortress
that is the Old Castle at Sherborne, before deciding that it would be
easier to build a new one. The magnificent Tudor mansion known
simply as Sherborne Castle is the result.

It was not only Raleigh who found the castle something of a challenge. Oliver Cromwell called it 'malicious and mischievous' when his forces under Fairfax took sixteen days to capture it during the Civil War, and it is of the castle at this period that Thomas Hardy writes in the tale of Lady Baxby in his collection of short stories, *A Group of Noble Dames* (1891). Following his usual practice, Hardy alters the castle's name, and it appears in his story as Sherton:

> It was in the time of the great Civil War—if I should not rather, as a loyal subject, call it, with Clarendon, the Great Rebellion. It was, I say, at that unhappy period of our history, that towards the autumn of a particular year, the Parliament forces sat down before Sherton Castle with over seven thousand foot and four pieces of cannon. The Castle, as we all know, was in that century owned and occupied by one of the Earls of Severn, and garrisoned for his assistance by a certain noble Marquis who commanded the King's troops in these parts. The said Earl, as well as the young Lord Baxby, his eldest son, were away from home just now, raising forces for the King elsewhere. But there were present in the Castle, when the besiegers arrived before it, the son's fair wife Lady Baxby, and her servants, together with some friends and near relatives of her husband; and the defence was so good and well-considered that they anticipated no great danger.

Hardy's tale relates to a siege a few years prior to the successful one by Fairfax, when the commander of the Parliamentary troops was Lady Baxby's brother, William. He tries to persuade her to join their cause, and her already strong inclination to do so is strengthened after her husband's return, when the two quarrel. Dressed in his clothes, she is on the point of secretly leaving the castle when a woman, clearly mistaking her for her husband, greets her suggestively.

Shocked at the possibility of her husband's infidelity, she returns to their bedroom and devises a cunning plan to thwart any nocturnal shenanigans: she places the key to the locked bedroom door beneath her pillow, ties a lock of her husband's hair to the bedpost with a lace from her stays, and takes a firm hold of his hand.

Of course, the good Lord Baxby has not been an unfaithful husband. The young woman had been trying her luck after a chance encounter the day before. But the misunderstanding has been a fortuitous one, and Lady Baxby's proposed desertion of king and spouse can remain her little secret.

LEFT The castle's massive defences were a challenge to Cromwell during the Civil War.

Maiden Castle

Man-made promontory it may be, but in the imagination of novelist John Cowper Powys Maiden Castle was also a huge prehistoric dungheap, or a vast tortoise, or a giant dinosaur's nest.

Powys had grown up in Dorchester, where his father was curate of St Peter's, but he spent much of his life in America before returning to live in the town again at the age of 62. Here he began work on his novel *Maiden Castle* (1936), which is set in the Dorchester of the time. It centres on the character of Dud No-man, a historical novelist in mourning for the death of the much-loved wife who had rejected him. He meets an itinerant circus acrobat, Wizzie, and the novel follows the efforts of this couple, and other interconnected characters, to accommodate themselves to each other's lives and worlds. In the background to the main plot archaeologists are digging at Maiden Castle, and the earthwork has a symbolic presence in the book:

> Dud stared in fascinated awe at the great earth-monument.
> From this halfway distance it took all sorts of strange forms to his shameless mind. It took the shape of a huge 'dropping' of supermammoth dung.
>
> It took the shape of an enormous seaweed-encrusted shell, the shell of the fish called Kraken, whom some dim motion of monstrous mate-lust had drawn up from the primeval slime of its seabed.
>
> It took the shape of that vast planetary Tortoise, upon whose curved back, sealed with the convoluted inscriptions of the Nameless Tao, rested the pillar of creation.
>
> But above all as he surveyed that dark-green bulk rising at the end of the long, narrow road he was compelled to think of the mysterious nest of some gigantic Jurassic-age bird-dragon, such as, in this May sunshine, he could imagine even now hatching its portentous egg.

Powys's theme is the difficulty – or as he sees it, the impossibility – of maintaining personal integrity in the context of modern society. Dud's story is ultimately one of failure, though having a father who believes himself to be the incarnation of an ancient Welsh god is a situation most of us would find challenging.

Whether he was a maligned genius or a literary dinosaur, there is no doubting Powys's descriptive originality.

John Cowper Powys, *unattributed photograph*

LEFT The vast earthworks at Maiden Castle, the largest Iron Age hillfort in Europe. Two hundred families could be accommodated within these protective ramparts.

Launceston Castle

It was very far from the intentions of George Fox, when he started to preach in fields and marketplaces in 1648, to found a new Christian sect. But a group of people who shared his views on the genuine principles of Christianity began to gather around him, and the Society of Friends, or Quakers, came into being.

Fox had been a serious child, but although his family recognised his spiritual inclinations, he was nevertheless apprenticed to a shoemaker. At the age of 19, dismayed to see clerical men out drinking, he felt drawn to lead a solitary life and become 'a stranger unto all'. He grew dissatisfied with the clergy he encountered, and came to feel that a genuine calling rather than an academic qualification was the making of a true priest.

During his ministry Fox was frequently arrested and imprisoned for unauthorised worship, and even for wearing his hat in court. In chapter nine of his autobiography, *A Visit to the Southern Counties Which Ends in Launceston Jail* (1655–6), his account of the conditions that he and his companions experienced while imprisoned at Launceston is explicit in its detail:

LEFT Launceston Castle is set on the high motte, or mound, of a Norman stronghold; it was built in the 12th century, replacing an earlier wooden structure.

> The assizes being over, and we settled in prison upon such a commitment that we were not likely to be soon released, we broke from giving the jailer 7 shillings a week apiece for our horses, and 7 shillings a week for ourselves, and sent our horses into the country. Upon which he grew very wicked and devilish, and put us down into Doomsdale, a nasty, stinking place, where they used to put murderers after they were condemned. The place was so noisome ... and the excrement of the prisoners ... had not been carried out for so many years. So that it was all like mire, and in some places to the tops of the shoes in water and urine ... At night, some friendly people of the town brought us a candle and a little straw ...

Later, the jailer even pours excrement down on their heads from above. Reading Fox's account of the Launceston dungeon, it is not hard to understand why the Quakers became such energetic prison reformers.

When Celia Fiennes writes of her visit to Launceston, or Lanston, to use her incorrigible spelling, her opening comment is that the 'wet and dirty lanes in many places made it a tedious journey'. But Celia is no delicate flower. She made her journeys through the length and breadth of England on horseback, and potholes in the path had been known to separate her rather too abruptly from her mount.

In the preface to her *Journeys*, Celia explains that they were undertaken 'to regain my health by variety and change of aire and exercise', and the journal, mostly written in 1702, was begun so that 'as my bodily health was promoted my mind should not appear totally unoccupied'.

The daughter of Colonel Nathaniel Fiennes, who had surrendered Bristol to Prince Rupert during the Civil War, Celia grew up close to the centre of Parliamentarian power, and it may be that travelling in this way expressed an inherent taste for a life of courage and adventure.

Celia's account of her visit to Launceston is typical of her energetic style and unconventional grammar:

> I could see none of the town till just as I was, as
> you may say, ready to tumble into it, there being a
> vast steep to descend to which the town seemed in
> a bottom yet I was forced to ascend a pretty good
> hill into the place.

Characteristically, she is aware of the town's ecclesiastical status, it being 'noe Citty' since the cathedral of its diocese is Exeter. The castle, though, does seem to make an impression:

> There is a great ascent upon into the Castle which
> looks very great and in good repaire, the walls and
> towers round it, its true there is but a part of it
> remains the round tower or fort being still standing
> and makes a good appearance.

Evidently Celia Fiennes's travels benefited her physical well-being enormously, or at least she believed they did. Writing her will at the age of 76, having visited every county in England, the intrepid lady declared herself to be 'in perfect health'.

Dartmouth Castle

A shipman was ther, wonynge fer by weste;
For aught I woot, he was of Dertemouthe.

In his introduction to the shipman, or sailor, in the Prologue to *The Canterbury Tales* (unfinished at the time of the author's death in 1400), Geoffrey Chaucer indicates that this member of the party hailed from Dartmouth. The shipman is said to have been based on John Hawley, mayor of Dartmouth when Chaucer visited the town and builder of the first castle to occupy this site. Chaucer describes him as 'a good felawe', and one who enjoys 'ful many a draughte of wyn'.

Chaucer's twenty-nine pilgrims are travelling from the Tabard Inn in Southwark to the grave of St Thomas à Becket in Canterbury, and to while away the hours each tells a tale. Given the nature of their journey these pilgrims tell some saucy stories, and the 'Shipman's Tale' is one of the cheekiest.

A merchant's wife needs money to buy some new clothes and persuades the priest to lend her 100 francs. The man of God is happy to oblige; he promptly borrows the money from the merchant, who is leaving on a business trip, and enjoys an energetic night in the woman's bed in return for the favour:

In myrthe al nyght a bisy lyf they lede.

When the merchant returns, the priest tells him that he has repaid the 100 francs to his wife, which she has to admit. But after his own night of passion ...

'Namoore,' quod she,' by God, ye have ynough!'

... the merchant forgives her for spending the money, and she promises to repay him with her 'joly body'.

Daniel Defoe remarks on the 'good strong fort' guarding the entrance to Dartmouth harbour in his three-volume guidebook, *A Tour thro' the Whole Island of Great Britain* (1724). Defoe's travels through the kingdom were often undertaken as fact-finding missions for the Tory politician who had rescued him from prison and penury

after various business and writing projects came to grief. Defoe's account of his visit describes the arrival of a huge school of pilchards in the harbour:

> I had the curiosity here ... to go out to the mouth of the haven in a boat to see the entrance, and castle or fort that commands it; and coming back with the tide of flood, I observed some small fish to skip and play upon the surface of the water ... Immediately one of the rowers or seamen starts up in the boat, and, throwing his arms abroad as if he had been bewitched, cries out as loud as he could bawl, 'A school! A school!'

According to Defoe, about 40,000 were netted by one small fishing boat alone, and he tells with relish how his evening meal of fresh pilchards, broiled at the inn, cost him only a farthing per head 'dressing and all'.

Defoe is delighted to find that good food is so much less expensive here than in London: a good lobster that would set him back at least three shillings in the capital could be found for as little as sixpence – a sixth of the price. Whatever his credentials as a spy, Defoe clearly had a good eye for a bargain.

ABOVE Dartmouth Castle was built in the 14th century to defend the Dart Estuary, along with the livelihood of the merchants who depended on these waters for their trade.

Grimspound, Hound Tor Medieval Village and Merrivale Prehistoric Settlement

When Sir Charles Baskerville is found dead in mysterious circumstances, Sherlock Holmes embarks on one of his most famous cases. The Baskerville family is haunted by the legend of a huge fire-breathing hound that killed an ancestor, the dastardly Hugh Baskerville, and was seen on the night of Sir Charles's death.

Holmes is determined to save the last of the Baskerville line, the affable Henry, from the strange bearded man who is following him around London, so he sends him, accompanied by Dr Watson, to the supposed safety of Baskerville Hall. Watson finds the middle of Dartmoor 'a rather uncanny place altogether', but he does his best to keep a protective eye on Henry and send reports back to Holmes in London. On his first expedition with Henry on to the moor, Watson is impressed by a strange sight:

LEFT Hound Tor: the remains of several farmsteads, abandoned in the Middle Ages, survive at this site, which was first occupied during the Bronze Age.

> The whole steep slope was covered with gray circular rings of stone, a score of them at least.
>
> 'What are they? Sheep-pens?'
>
> 'No, they are the homes of our worthy ancestors. Prehistoric man lived thickly on the moor, and as no one in particular has lived there since, we find all his little arrangements exactly as he left them. These are his wigwams with the roofs off. You can even see his hearth and his couch if you have the curiosity to go inside.'
>
> 'But it is quite a town. When was it inhabited?'
>
> 'Neolithic man – no date.'
>
> 'What did he do?'
>
> 'He grazed his cattle on these slopes, and he learned to dig for tin when the bronze sword began to supersede the stone axe. Look at the great trench in the opposite hill. That is his mark.'

This description by Sir Arthur Conan Doyle in his *Hound of the Baskervilles* (1902) relates to Grimspound and Merrivale, settlements that actually date from the Bronze Age, and Hound Tor, a deserted medieval village first occupied in the Bronze Age. Watson is strongly affected by these places, and he writes to Holmes:

On all sides of you as you walk are the houses of these long forgotten folk, with their graves and the huge monoliths which are supposed to have marked their temples. As you look at their gray stone huts against the scarred hillsides you leave your own age behind you, and if you were to see a skin-clad, hairy man crawl out from the low door, fitting a flint-tipped arrow on to the string of his bow, you would feel that his presence there was more natural than your own.

As well as a hound lurking on the moor there is also a dangerous convict and a tall stranger. And at Baskerville Hall, Barrymore the butler is behaving very strangely. It turns out that he is sending supplies, including cast-off clothes, to the convict, who happens to be his brother-in-law, but his assistance goes awry when the unfortunate chap is killed in mistake for Henry, whose clothes he was wearing. Watson, following information offered by the butler, hopes to impress Holmes by discovering the identity and whereabouts of the suspect stranger:

Barrymore's only indication had been that the stranger lived in one of these abandoned huts, and many hundreds of them are scattered throughout the length and breadth of the moor. But I had my own experience for a guide since it had shown me the man himself standing upon the summit of the Black Tor.

While Watson is examining signs of recent occupation in one of the huts, he is startled by the sudden return of the inhabitant. But far from the 'hairy man' of his imagination, it is none other than Holmes himself.

With the master now in attendance, the crime is quickly solved. Henry is saved from the machinations of a neighbour who turns out to be another Baskerville hoping to inherit the family fortune, and whose application of luminous paint to an enormous dog has been responsible for the strange sightings on the moor.

Although Conan Doyle furnishes a practical explanation for the other-worldly hound of his story, he was intensely interested in spiritualism and supernatural phenomena, attending seances and publicly declaring his belief in fairies. He even famously performed his own magic trick, resurrecting Sherlock Holmes from the dead when his reading public demanded further stories.

If he succumbed to some of the fads of his era, Conan Doyle also exemplified its values of loyalty and devotion. When his wife Louise was ill with tuberculosis he met and fell in love with a woman named Jean Leckie, but remained 'just friends' with her for ten years until his wife's death in 1906. He and Jean were married the following year.

Tintagel Castle

One of the most popular books of the Middle Ages was a vast historical romance by a 12th-century Benedictine monk, Geoffrey of Monmouth. Geoffrey's *Historia Regum Britanniae*, or *History of the Kings of Britain*, purported to be an accurate account of British monarchs from the mythical Brutus, great grandson of Trojan Aeneas, to the last of the British kings, Cadwallader, in the 7th century, but scholars have long believed it to be more a work of fiction than of fact. The central figure in Geoffrey's narrative is Arthur, and his spirited account of the legendary king's life and exploits has influenced and inspired subsequent visions of Camelot by Malory, Tennyson and Swinburne, not to mention Hollywood and Monty Python.

According to Geoffrey, Uther Pendragon, king of the Britons, called his nobles to a great feast, and there fell in love with the beautiful Ygerna. Ygerna's husband, the Duke of Cornwall, did not welcome Uther's attentions to his wife, and leaving the feast without taking leave, stowed her in the safest place he could think of, Tintagel Castle. Uther gave siege, but in an agony of desire for Ygerna he turned to his friend, Ulfin:

> 'You must tell me how I can satisfy my desire for her, for otherwise I shall die of the passion which is consuming me.'
> 'Who can possibly give you useful advice,' answered Ulfin, 'when no power on earth can enable us to come to her where she is inside the fortress of Tintagel? The castle is built high above the sea, which surrounds it on all sides, and there is no other way in except that offered by a narrow isthmus of rock. Three armed soldiers could hold it against you, even if you stood there with the whole kingdom of Britain at your side.'

However, it occurred to Ulfin that Merlin might be of help, and sure enough the 'prophet' enabled Uther to gain admittance to the lady's chamber by transforming him, with the aid of a special potion, into the likeness of Ygerna's husband. That night Arthur was conceived, and the Duke of Cornwall killed. The happy Uther then lived with Ygerna for the rest of his days.

The 15th-century author Sir Thomas Malory composed his expansive account of the Arthurian legends, *Le Morte D'Arthur*, while serving the longest of his several prison sentences. The knight Malory's life seems to have been full of adventure in its own right: among the charges brought against him were theft and rape – indeed, the rape of the same married woman on two occasions – and he twice effected daring escapes from prison. So the salty account of the pursuit of Igrayne by Uther may well owe something to the knight's personal experiences. Uther is described as 'wonderly wrothe' when the woman he desires leaves his feast without permission and Malory frequently enlivens the tale with dialogue, as here when Merlin explains his plan to Uther:

> 'Syre,' said Merlyn, 'this is my desire: the first night that ye shal lye by Igrayne ye shal gete a child on her; and whan that is borne, that it shal be delyverd to me for to nourisshe thereas I wille have it, for it shal be your worship and the childis availe as mykel as the child is worth.'
> 'I wylle wel,' said the kynge, 'as thow wilt have it.'
> 'Now make you redy,' said Merlyn. 'This nyght ye shalle lye with Igrayne in the castel of Tyntigayll.'

With these 12th- and 15th-century tomes much in mind, Alfred, Lord Tennyson, the Poet Laureate, wrote his poem sequence *Idylls of the King*, the first four poems in the sequence being published in 1859. This was immensely popular at the time, selling 10,000 copies in six weeks, though subsequent critics, including Swinburne, were less than enthusiastic. The sequence begins with the meeting of Arthur and Guinevere and ends with Arthur's last great battle at Lyonesse, the legendary kingdom lost beneath the waves in the far west of Cornwall. Here, he defeats – but meets his death at the hand of – Modred, whom Geoffrey of Monmouth identifies as Arthur's son from an incestuous union with Morgause, his sister:

> Then rose the King and moved his host by night,
> And ever push'd Sir Modred, league by league,
> Back to the sunset bound of Lyonesse—
> A land of old upheaven from the abyss
> By fire, to sink into the abyss again;
> Where fragments of forgotten peoples dwelt,
> And the long mountains ended in a coast
> Of ever-shifting sand, and far away
> The phantom circle of a moaning sea.

As he dies, Arthur refers to Merlin's prediction that he will 'come again/To rule once more' – the once and future king.

Tennyson's contemporary Algernon Charles Swinburne encountered these legends when, in 1857, he met the future Pre-Raphaelite trio, Rossetti, Morris and Burne-Jones, at Oxford, where they were busy painting Arthurian murals on the walls of the Oxford Union. Swinburne visited Tintagel in the early autumn of 1864, and here completed *Atalanta in Corydon*, the first work to be published in his name. However, the poem that has Tintagel as its setting, and that Swinburne considered to be his masterpiece, did not appear for nearly twenty years. *Tristram of Lyonesse* (1882) narrates the other tragic love triangle of Arthurian legend: that of Tristram, Isolt and King Mark. Isolt, betrothed to King Mark, is escorted from her native Ireland by Mark's nephew, Tristram:

ABOVE **Inside Merlin's Cave in the cliff below the castle.**

> To the loud rocks and ringing reaches home
> That take the wild wrath of the Cornish foam,
> Past Lyonesse unswallowed of the tide
> And high Carlion that now the steep sea hides
> To the wind-hollowed heights and gusty bays
> Of sheer Tintagel, fair with famous days.

On the journey the couple mistakenly drink a love potion intended for Isolt and Mark, and are doomed to an eternal love for each other that, since Isolt must fulfil her duty and marry Mark, can only be contrived through deceit and subterfuge.

Five centuries after Malory, T H White reworked the errant knight's vast narrative in a group of novels collected as *The Once and Future King* (1958). The musical *Camelot* is based on White's books, and the first of the four, *The Sword in the Stone* (1938), inspired the 1963 animated film of the same name. The book itself is a children's classic, a funny and touching tale of young Arthur's education by Merlin. Like the wizard he brought so vividly to the page, White was to pursue his own journey – a literary one – backwards in time, beyond Malory to the era of Geoffrey of Monmouth, when he translated a 12th-century Latin bestiary, *The Book of Beasts*.

Goodrich Castle

Thomas, grandfather of the satirist Jonathan Swift, became vicar of Goodrich in 1628. A zealous Royalist, Thomas mortgaged his estate to raise money for the beleaguered Charles I, later forfeiting his living and enduring imprisonment as a result. Thomas carried with him a chalice for celebrating Eucharist, which on his death passed to Jonathan, and in 1726, the year in which *Gulliver's Travels* appeared, Swift dedicated it to the service of Goodrich church in perpetuity.

Man of God he may have been, but Swift wielded a wicked pen. Three years later he published *A Modest Proposal*, his pamphlet advocating a 'cheap, easy and effectual' method of alleviating the sufferings of the Irish poor: fattening their children for use as food. It is regarded as a satirical masterpiece.

In 1798, William Wordsworth and Samuel Taylor Coleridge were preparing their groundbreaking collection *Lyrical Ballads*. This was to include Coleridge's seafaring rhyme *The Ancient Mariner*:

> It is an ancient Mariner,
> And he stoppeth one of three.
> 'By thy long grey beard and glittering eye
> Now wherefore stopp'st thou me? ...'

Along with some other shorter poems, Wordsworth's contribution to the supernatural theme of the volume was his poem *We Are Seven*. He had met the little girl who was to be the inspiration for this poem five years earlier, in 1793, on his first visit to Goodrich Castle during a lengthy walking tour:

> I met a little cottage Girl:
> She was eight years old, she said;
> Her hair was thick with many a curl
> That clustered round her head.
>
> She had a rustic woodland air,
> And she was wildly clad:
> Her eyes were fair, and very fair;
> Her beauty made me glad ...

In his detailed account of the writing of this poem, Wordsworth tells how a friend entreated him to withdraw *We Are Seven* from publication, fearing that it would make him 'everlastingly ridiculous'. The request was cheerfully denied.

Wordsworth returned to Goodrich Castle in 1841, hoping to find some trace of the little person. But the experience was a disappointment:

> The ruin, from its position and features, is a most impressive object. I could not but deeply regret that its solemnity was impaired by a fantastic new Castle set up on a projection of the same ridge, as if to show how far modern art can go in surpassing all that could be done by antiquity and nature with their united graces ...

Wordsworth never did find his poetic inspiration. But this is hardly surprising when, as he says himself, he 'did not even know her name'.

ABOVE **Goodrich Castle** stands high above the River Wye on a red sandstone crag. It is likely that the rectangular keep was built very early in the 12th century, while the outer walls are the remains of a later, 13th-century, structure.

Wroxeter Roman City, Buildwas Abbey and Clun Castle

A E Housman was born and grew up near Bromsgrove, Worcestershire, but always had 'a sentimental feeling for Shropshire because its hills were our western horizon'. A brilliant Latin scholar, Housman failed his finals at Oxford, but published articles on classical authors during his ten years as clerk at the Patent Office in London.

It was when his dearest friend Moses Jackson emigrated and married in 1887 that Housman began experimenting with poetry. In 1896 his self-published volume *A Shropshire Lad*, containing sixty-three untitled verses mostly based on a ballad form, met with little immediate enthusiasm.

In one of the most evocative of the poems, Housman imagines winds blowing through the ancient Roman city of Wroxeter, *Viroconium Cornoviorum* or *Uricon*:

On Wenlock Edge the wood's in trouble;
His forest fleece the Wrekin heaves;
The gale, it plies the saplings double,
And thick on Severn snow the leaves.

'Twould blow like this through holt and hanger
When Uricon the city stood:
'Tis the old wind in the old anger,
But then it threshed another wood.

Then, 'twas before my time, the Roman
At yonder heaving hill would stare:
The blood that warms the English yeoman,
The thoughts that hurt him, they were there.

There, like the wind through woods in riot,
Through him the gale of life blew high;
The tree of man was never quiet:
Then 'twas the Roman, now 'tis I.

The gale, it plies the saplings double,
It blows so hard 'twill soon be gone:
To-day the Roman and his trouble
Are ashes under Uricon.

LEFT Remains of the municipal baths at Wroxeter Roman City. The hypocaust, the Romans' under-floor heating system, is visible in the foreground.

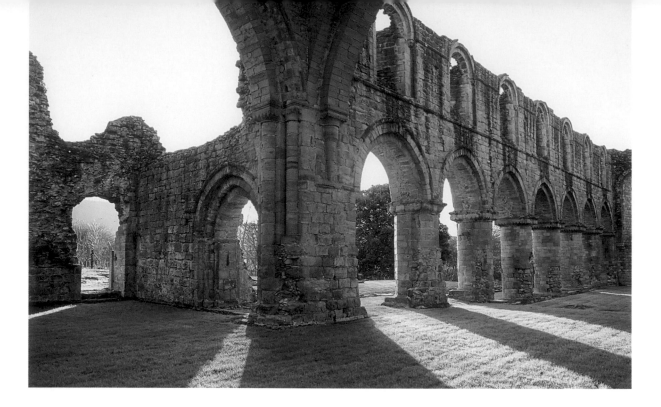

Housman's sense of place does not depend on a detailed description of nature; he is recreating landscapes of the mind and of the past with a broad brush, as here when contemplating the ancient feuding in the Welsh Marches:

> Ages since the vanquished bled
> Round my mother's marriage-bed;
> There the ravens feasted far
> About the open house of war:
>
> When Severn down to Buildwas ran
> Coloured with the death of man,
> Couched upon her brother's grave
> The Saxon got me on the slave ...
>
> In my heart it has not died,
> The war that sleeps on Severn side;
> They cease not fighting east and west,
> On the marches of my breast.

LEFT Clun Castle, close to the border with Wales, is silhouetted by the setting sun.

It is easy to see how these verses struck a chord with the young men in the trenches of the First World War, when Housman's late-Victorian vision of 'a land of lost content' became enormously popular:

> Clunton and Clunbury,
> Clungunford and Clun,
> Are the quietest places
> Under the sun.

The writer of these gentle rhythmic verses became a professor of Latin in 1892 and several subsequent volumes of poetry were published. But when Jackson died in 1923, Housman's poetry ceased.

Clun Castle may be the model for Garde Doloureuse in *The Betrothed*, a novel by **Sir Walter Scott**, part of which was written during his stay in Clun. Although all the action of the book takes place in the Welsh Marches it was grouped with *The Talisman* as *Tales of the Crusaders* (1825) – the tenuous link being that the novel's heroine is betrothed to an absent crusader – because Scott's publishers thought it would be a commercial failure if published alone. The author did not disagree with their judgement.

Kenilworth Castle

The castle at Kenilworth was substantially enlarged between 1389 and 1394 by John of Gaunt, who rebuilt the great hall and added private apartments overlooking the lake. Gaunt, Duke of Lancaster and chief counsellor and uncle to the young King Richard II, was the most powerful nobleman in England. But Gaunt and Richard later became bitter enemies and, in Shakespeare's *Richard II*, the king seizes Gaunt's property. Gaunt is given Shakespeare's most rousing patriotic speech in Act 2 of the play:

> This royal throne of kings, this sceptred isle,
> This earth of majesty, this seat of Mars,
> This other Eden, demi-paradise,
> This fortress built by nature for herself
> Against infection and the hand of war,
> This happy breed of men, this little world,
> This precious stone set in the silver sea
> Which serves it in the office of a wall
> Or as a moat defensive to a house
> Against the envy of less happier lands,
> This blessed plot, this earth, this realm, this England ...

ABOVE The extensive ruins at Kenilworth Castle include an impressive Norman keep and John of Gaunt's great hall.

Gaunt's eloquent concern for the state of England is soon answered; his son is Henry Bolingbroke, who subsequently takes Richard's crown and sends him to the Tower. The ineffectual Richard finally comes to a bloody end at Pomfret Castle.

Kenilworth came into the possession of the Dudley family in the 16th century, but was forfeited when Dudley was executed in 1553 for his attempt to place Lady Jane Grey, his daughter-in-law, on the throne. However, John's son Robert, Earl of Leicester, was a favourite of Elizabeth I, so Kenilworth was restored to the family and Elizabeth was often entertained here by Leicester in great style.

LEFT Robert Dudley, Earl of Leicester, added these extensions to the castle in the Tudor period.

It is this heyday in the castle's history that Sir Walter Scott recreates in the final spectacular scenes of his novel *Kenilworth*. Published in 1821, the year of the coronation of George IV, the book is a vivid depiction of the Elizabethan age, with Shakespeare, Spenser and Raleigh all making appearances. Scott's tale centres on the secret marriage of Robert Dudley to Amy Robsart, whom he keeps a virtual prisoner in the country, hoping to avoid discovery and thereby maintain his special place at court. When Tressilian, Amy's former fiancé, goes in pursuit, Dudley's Master of the Horse, Varney, tries to shield his patron by swearing that Amy is actually *his* wife. The queen orders Varney to bring Amy to the revels at Kenilworth, and after foiling his plan to poison her, Amy makes her own way to the castle, to seek help from her true husband:

> At length the princely castle appeared, upon improving which, and the domains around, the Earl of Leicester had, it is said, expended sixty thousand pounds sterling ...
>
> The outer wall ... enclosed seven acres, a part of which was occupied by extensive stables, and by a pleasure garden, with its trim arbours and parterres, and the rest formed the base-court, or outer yard, of the noble castle.
>
> The lordly structure itself, which rose near the centre of this spacious enclosure, was composed of a huge pile of magnificent castellated buildings, apparently of different ages, surrounding an inner court ... A large and massive keep, which formed the citadel of the castle, was of uncertain though great antiquity ...
>
> The external wall of this royal castle was, on the south and west sides, adorned and defended by a lake partly artificial, across which Leicester had constructed a stately bridge, that Elizabeth might enter the castle by a path hitherto untrodden ...

Scott characteristically balances this verbal reconstruction with the state of the castle at the time of writing, before returning to his ill-fated heroine:

> The bed of the lake is but a rushy swamp; and the massive ruins of the castle only serve to show what their splendour once was, and to impress on the musing visitor the transitory value of human possessions ...
>
> It was with far different feelings that the unfortunate Countess of Leicester viewed those gray and massive towers, when she first beheld them rise above the embowering and richly shaded woods ...

The Queen has a very different experience on entering the castle through Mortimer's Tower, and going on into the great hall, which is hung with 'silken tapestry, blazing with torches, misty with perfumes, and sounding to strains of soft and delicious music'.

Unfortunately for Amy, she encounters Elizabeth before she can make contact with Leicester, and through misunderstanding and betrayal the story ends tragically for all except Elizabeth and Leicester. Not surprisingly, *Kenilworth* was an immediate success.

ABOVE View of the Tudor garden in front of the Norman keep.

Furness Abbey and Piel Castle

The area around Furness was first explored by William Wordsworth when he was a schoolboy at Hawkshead Grammar School. He had moved there from Penrith to continue his education after the death of his mother in 1778, and in his long autobiographical poem *The Prelude* (1805), he recalls how he and a friend hired horses and set out towards Furness Abbey:

RIGHT **St Mary of Furness,** first founded in 1123 by Stephen, later king of England. The buildings were remodelled in the 15th century and it is from this period that these dramatic ruins survive.

> ... a structure famed
> Beyond its neighbourhood, the antique walls
> Of that large abbey which within the Vale
> Of Nightshade, to St Mary's honour built,
> Stands yet a mouldering pile with fractured arch,
> Belfry, and images, and living trees,
> A holy scene!

But young Wordsworth's purpose was neither religious nor cultural:

> Through the walls we flew
> And down the valley, and, a circuit made
> In wantonness of heart, through rough and smooth
> We scampered homeward.

After his student days at St John's College, Cambridge, Wordsworth returned to the area in 1794 to join his sister Dorothy, who was staying with cousins at Rampside, a village on the edge of Morecambe Bay. He explored the sands and visited Piel Castle, but it was not until 1805, prompted by Sir George Beaumont's painting of the castle, that he put his response into words:

I was thy neighbour once, thou rugged Pile!
Four summer weeks I dwelt in sight of thee:
I saw thee every day; and all the while,
Thy form was sleeping on a glassy sea.

Much later in life, in his seventies, Wordsworth returned to Furness to find the Furness Railway Company laying its line through the abbey grounds, an experience that prompted his sonnet *At Furness Abbey* (1844). Wordsworth campaigned to prevent the railway's advance through the area, and his sonnet concludes with a direct address to the local landowner, Lord Cavendish:

ABOVE Piel Castle, whose reflection Wordsworth observed in the waters of the Irish sea, close by the harbour at Barrow-in-Furness.

Here, where, of havoc tired and rash undoing,
Man left this Structure to become Time's prey
A soothing spirit follows in the way
That Nature takes, her counter-work pursuing.
See how her Ivy clasps the sacred Ruin
Fall to prevent or beautify decay;
And, on the mouldered walls, how bright, how gay,
The flowers in pearly dews their bloom renewing!
Thanks to the place, blessings upon the hour;
Even as I speak the rising Sun's first smile
Gleams on the grass-crowned top of yon tall Tower
Whose cawing occupants with joy proclaim
Prescriptive title to the shattered pile
Where, Cavendish, 'thine' seems nothing but a name!

Brougham Castle

Penrith was home to William Wordsworth when he was a young child. His rather stern maternal grandparents lived in the town, and he attended a dame school there until his mother's death in 1778. But this event divided the young family: William and his brothers were sent to school in Hawkshead and sister Dorothy to live with relatives in Halifax.

After his father died in 1783 Wordsworth again spent time in the town, passing the school holidays in the care of his uncle. But the two did not find each other easy company, and William was glad when his sister Dorothy moved back to Penrith in 1787. During that summer they explored the local countryside, visiting the ruins of Brougham Castle and renewing their friendship with Mary Hutchinson, whom Wordsworth married in 1802.

Following his poetic credo that verse should be 'emotion recollected in tranquillity', it was not until twenty years after their summer visit that Wordsworth wrote his *Song at the Feast of Brougham Castle* with its rousing opening lines:

William Wordsworth, chalk drawing by Benjamin Robert Haydon, 1818.

> High in the breathless Hall the Minstrel sate,
> And Emont's murmur mingled with the Song.
> The words of ancient time I thus translate,
> A festal strain that hath been silent long ...

The poem's subtitle – *Upon the restoration of Lord Clifford, the shepherd, to the estates and honours of his ancestors* – refers to a traditional legend about the Cliffords of Brougham from the time of the Wars of the Roses. When Lancastrian supporter John, Lord Clifford, killed the young Yorkist Earl of Rutland at the Battle of Wakefield and was subsequently killed himself at Towton, his widow Margaret feared for her son's safety, and sent him to be reared by a shepherd. Henry Clifford grew to manhood without any knowledge of his lineage, and when the Lancastrians finally regained the throne after the Battle of Bosworth, he was restored as Lord Clifford, with all the estates that had been forfeited by his father. Aged 32 and illiterate, the restored shepherd-lord was a perfect subject for Wordsworth's imagination, and his passionate belief in nature as a moral teacher:

Love had he found in huts where poor men lie;
His daily teachers had been woods and rills,
The silence that is in the starry sky,
The sleep that is among the lonely hills.

In him the savage virtue of the Race,
Revenge, and all ferocious thoughts were dead:
Nor did he change; but kept in lofty place
The wisdom which adversity had bred.

Absent here is Wordsworth's propensity to address with exclamatory language every 'lofty pile', and the *Song* concludes with some of his most lyrical and touching lines.

Hadrian's Wall

Life for the legionary serving at the far reaches of the Roman Empire was in many ways a comfortable and sociable affair, according to fragments of writing tablets excavated at Vindolanda, the Roman fort beside Hadrian's Wall at Chesterholm. A variety of texts, from domestic accounts and receipts to medical prescriptions and personal letters, preserved on wooden tablets, have been discovered at the site since the start of excavation work in 1973. The fragments include the first line of the *Aeneid*, the poem by Virgil (unfinished at his death in 19 BC) that tells the story of the founding of Rome by Aeneas after the sack of Troy:

> Arma virumque cano Troiae qui primus ab oris
> (I sing of arms and the man who first from the shores of Troy ...)

This was a famous quotation throughout the empire, probably used for writing practice, like our 'Quick brown fox ...' sentence today. A letter from Flavius Cerialis to Crispius, who had apparently introduced him to some influential people, gives a positive image of life at the fort:

> Thanks to you I may be able to enjoy a pleasant period of
> military service. I write this to you from Vindolanda where my
> winter quarters are.

Lists of foodstuffs include roe deer, young pig, venison and spices, and there are requests for deliveries of oysters and Massic wine, a highly reputed Italian vintage. Household accounts indicate the use of a sophisticated range of culinary utensils including side plates, egg cups and bread baskets.

Domestic bliss was very much in the mind of Sir Walter Scott when he visited Hadrian's Wall in 1797, because it was here, in the North Pennine village of Gilsland, at the 'Popping Stone' – a traditional place to 'pop the question' – that he proposed to Charlotte Carpentier.

Scott had fallen in love with Williamina Belsches in 1790 and throughout his subsequent training and practice as a lawyer he had hopes that she would accept him. But in 1797 she married another man and the heartbroken Scott, trying to forget his disappointment on a visit to the Lake District, met Charlotte. Mademoiselle Carpentier accepted his proposal, and they were married a few months later at Carlisle Cathedral.

To a Lady
With flowers from the Roman Wall

Take these flowers which, purple waving,
  On the ruin'd rampart grew,
Where, the sons of freedom braving,
Rome's imperial standards flew.

Warriors from the breach of danger
  Pluck no longer laurels there;
They but yield the passing stranger
  Wild-flower wreaths for Beauty's hair.

ABOVE The emperor Hadrian built his wall to defend the northernmost boundary of Roman Britain in about AD 122. This fine stretch of wall is at Cawfields, just north of Haltwhistle in Northumberland.

A Roman centurion is one of the characters Puck conjures up to entertain Dan and Una in *Puck of Pook's Hill* (1906). In this novel by Rudyard Kipling Parnesius tells the children that 'old men who have followed the Eagles since boyhood say nothing in the Empire is more wonderful than first sight of the Wall':

> Along the top are towers with guard-houses, small towers, between. Even on the narrowest part of it three men with shields can walk abreast, from guard-house to guard-house. A little curtain wall, no higher than a man's neck, runs along the top of the thick wall, so that from a distance you see the helmets of the sentries sliding back and forth like beads. Thirty feet high is the Wall, and on the Picts' side, the North, is a ditch, strewn with blades of old swords and spear-heads set in wood, and tyres of wheels joined by chains.

Kipling, with his reputation as the poet of empire, refused many honours, but he accepted the Nobel Prize for Literature in 1907, the year after *Puck* was published. He was the first English writer to receive it.

Heroic and romantic visions of Hadrian's Wall are challenged by W H Auden in *Roman Wall Blues* (1937), a poem from his *Twelve Songs*:

> Over the heather the wet wind blows,
> I've lice in my tunic and a cold in my nose.
>
> The rain comes pattering out of the sky,
> I'm a Wall soldier, I don't know why.
>
> The mist creeps over the hard grey stone,
> My girl's in Tungria; I sleep alone.
>
> Aulus goes hanging around her place,
> I don't like his manners, I don't like his face.
>
> Piso's a Christian, he worships a fish;
> There'd be no kissing if he had his wish.
>
> She gave me a ring but I diced it away;
> I want my girl and I want my pay.
>
> When I'm a veteran with only one eye
> I shall do nothing but look at the sky.

W H Auden,
photograph by Howard Coster, 1937.

Always interested in the private experience within the public sphere, Auden imagines a bleak life for his soldier on the wall, though he himself loved the surrounding North Pennine landscape. Soldiering certainly never appealed to him, and although his socialist views led him to visit Spain in support of the Republicans during the Civil War, he chose to spend the Second World War years in America, where he was increasingly drawn to Christianity. Here he met his lifelong partner Chester Kallman, and he became an American citizen in 1946.

Despite Auden's grim picture, many soldiers at the wall made homes and raised families. Rosemary Sutcliff presents the real dangers faced by the legions, as well as the experiences of the Romans who decided to stay, in her children's novel *The Eagle of the Ninth* (1954). Marcus and his slave Esca set off into the unknown territory beyond the wall in an attempt to discover the fate of the Ninth Hispana Legion, which disappeared with the loss of 4,000 men. Marcus is the son of the commander of the legion's First Cohort, and he hopes to recover the Legion's Eagle and return it to Rome. Sutcliff creates a vivid picture of the Roman outpost:

> From Luguvallium in the west to Segedunum in the east, the Wall ran, leaping along with the jagged contours of the land; a great gash of stonework, still raw with newness. Eighty miles of fortresses, mile-castles, watch-towers, strung on one great curtain wall, and backed by the vallum ditch and the coast-to-coast Legionary road; and huddled along its southern side, the low sprawl of wine shops, temples, married quarters, and markets that always gathered in the wake of the Legions. A great and never-ceasing smother of noise: voices, marching feet, turning wheels, the ring of hammer on armourer's anvil, the clear calling of trumpets over all. This was the great Wall of Hadrian, shutting out the menace of the north.

Marcus discovers the fate of his father's cohort and the Eagle is found, but his quest has an unexpected ending: he meets a girl, and decides not to go home. *The Eagle of the Ninth* is the first in a trilogy about Roman Britain, the second volume following the lives of Marcus's Romano-British descendants.

Norham Castle, Lindisfarne Priory, Dunstanburgh Castle and Warkworth Castle

Although **Sir Walter Scott** is better known to us as a historical novelist, in his day he was a poet who enjoyed much greater popularity than his contemporary, Wordsworth. He was fascinated by the tales and ballads of the border country, and his long narrative poem *Marmion* (1808) is set in the countryside he knew well.

Marmion follows the adventures of its eponymous hero, opening with his arrival at Norham Castle and concluding at Flodden Field in 1513, at the battle between Henry VIII's forces and those of his brother-in-law, James IV of Scotland:

> Day set on Norham's castled steep,
> And Tweed's fair river, broad and deep,
> And Cheviot's mountains lone:
> The battled towers, the donjon keep,
> The loophole grates, where captives weep,
> The flanking walls that round it sweep,
> In yellow lustre shone …

A favourite of Henry VIII, Marmion is not a straightforward hero; he betrays one woman and pursues another for her property and power, before dying of his wounds on the battlefield.

The second of *Marmion's* six cantos follows the fate of Constance de Beverley, Marmion's betrayed lover and a nun who has broken her vows. It begins with a detailed description of a sea journey by the abbess of Whitby and five nuns northwards along the Northumbrian coast to Lindisfarne Priory, a journey Scott knew and loved:

> And now the vessel skirts the strand
> Of mountainous Northumberland;
> Towns, towers, and halls, successive rise,
> And catch the nuns' delighted eyes …
>
> Then did the Alne attention claim,
> And Warkworth, proud of Percy's name;
> And next, they cross'd themselves, to hear
> The whitening breakers sound so near,
> Where, boiling through the rocks, they roar
> On Dunstanborough's cavern'd shore …

The abbess arrives at the priory, 'a solemn, huge, and dark-red pile/Placed on the margin of the isle', where she has been summoned to preside at an inquisition to decide the fate of Constance. Scott relishes his description of the Holy Island architecture:

> In Saxon strength that Abbey frown'd,
> With massive arches broad and round,
> That rose alternate, row on row,
> On ponderous columns, short and low,
> Built ere the art was known,
> By pointed aisle, and shafted stalk,
> The arcades of an alley'd walk
> To emulate in stone.

But nothing Constance says in her spirited defence to the 'vassal slaves of bloody Rome' can save her from the inevitable sentence for a perjured nun, and both she and her accomplice are walled up alive in the priory. Scott's now proverbial couplet from the sixth canto of the poem sums up the unfortunate woman's fate:

> O what a tangled web we weave,
> When first we practise to deceive!

It was St Cuthbert who had led the conversion of Lindisfarne Priory from the Celtic to the Roman rite after the Synod of Whitby, and a vision he had while tending sheep is described by the Venerable Bede in his *Life and Miracles of St Cuthbert, Bishop of Lindisfarne* (721): 'he saw a long stream of light break through the darkness of the night, and in the midst of it a company of the heavenly host descended to the earth …'.

Although he was prior, Cuthbert preferred a hermit's life, and Bede describes the cell on the island of Farne which the monk had constructed for himself:

> The building is almost of a round form, from wall to wall about
> four or five poles in extent. The wall on the outside is higher than
> a man, but within, by excavating the rock, he made it much
> deeper to prevent the eyes and the thoughts from wandering.

Such was Cuthbert's reputation as a holy man that he was elected bishop of the Lindisfarne see, but he was unwilling to leave his blessed isolation on the island, until the king himself arrived and pleaded with him. Then, according to Bede:

> They drew him away from his retirement with tears in his eyes
> and took him to the synod. When he arrived there, although
> much resisting, he was overcome by the unanimous hush of all,
> and compelled to submit to undertake the duties of the bishopric.

Bede had been prompted to write his *Life* when Cuthbert's body was removed from Lindisfarne to protect it from the invading Vikings, and found to have remained undecayed. Four centuries after his death Cuthbert's body was apparently still intact, and in his footnotes to *Marmion*, Scott gives a humorous summary of Cuthbert's posthumous journeying:

The saint was a most capricious fellow-traveller; which was the more intolerable, as, like Sinbad's Old Man of the Sea, he journeyed upon the shoulders of his companions. They paraded him through Scotland for several years ... whence they attempted to sail for Ireland, but were driven back by tempests. He at length made a halt at Norham; from thence he went to Melrose, where he remained stationary for a short time, and then caused himself to be launched upon the Tweed in a stone coffin ...

Scott's reference in the poem to Warkworth Castle links it firmly to the family who supported Bolingboke, later Henry IV, in Shakespeare's *Richard II*: the Percys. The young Percy, son to the Duke of Northumberland, offers his allegiance to the future king:

My gracious lord, I tender you my service,
Such as it is, being tender, raw and young,
Which elder days will ripen and confirm
To more approved service and desert.

An Elizabethan audience would have been aware that the Percys went on to lead a rebellion against him some years later. In reality, young Percy, or Harry Hotspur, was two years older than Bolingbroke, but Shakespeare makes him much younger in *Richard II* and he becomes the rival of Bolingbroke's son Prince Hal in the sequel play, *Henry IV, Part 1*. In that most galling of scenarios for a young man, Hal is unfavourably compared to Hotspur by his own father, who is:

In envy that my Lord Northumberland
Should be the father to so blest a son,
A son who is the theme of honour's tongue;
Amongst a grove, the very straightest plant;
Who is sweet Fortune's minion and her pride …

But Hal later reveals his better qualities whilst the headstrong Hotspur turns traitor. Henry offers an amnesty to those who lay down their arms before the impending battle, but Hotspur is unaware of this and faces the prospect of death with courage, spurred on by recalling the Percy family motto:

Now, Esperance! Percy! and set on.
Sound all the lofty instruments of war,
And by that music let us all embrace …

But 'Esperance', or Hope, is not enough to alter young Percy's fate. Where Henry and Hal have become closer, Percy and his father are divided because Northumberland is too ill to fight alongside his son, and Shakespeare concludes the play with Hotspur being killed by Hal at the Battle of Shrewsbury.

BELOW A majestic hilltop stronghold, Warkworth Castle was home to the powerful Percy family.

St Paul's Monastery

The best account we have of the early history of England was written at St Paul's Monastery by a monk who lived there all his life. The **Venerable Bede** writes in his *Ecclesiastical History of the English People* (731) about the period between the raids of Julius Caesar in 54 BC and the arrival of St Augustine, the first missionary from Rome, in 597. He also concludes his five-volume work with a brief account of his own life:

*The Venerable Bede,
engraving by André Thevet, 1584.*

> At the age of seven I was by the care of my
> relations, given to the most reverend Abbot
> Benedict ... to be educated. From that time I have
> spent the whole of my life within that monastery,
> devoting all my pains to the study of the Scriptures,
> and amid the observance of monastic discipline ...
> it has been ever my delight to learn or teach or
> write. In my nineteenth year I was admitted to the
> diaconate, in my thirtieth to the priesthood.

Bede benefited from the large library of books which Benedict had assembled in the monastery, always acknowledging any passages he had taken from the writings of others. He writes as a staunch Northumbrian, but with the edification of his readers very much in mind:

> For if history records good things of good men, the
> thoughtful hearer is encouraged to imitate what is
> good; or if it records evil of wicked men, the good,
> religious reader or listener is encouraged to avoid
> all that is sinful and perverse.

His famous account of the Synod of Whitby in 664 may be questioned by modern scholars for its focus on the emotional debate about establishing Easter as a movable feast, but nevertheless his *History* is now, thirteen centuries after it was written, a best-selling religious paperback. In addition to this extensive work, Bede also wrote biography, most notably a *Life of St Cuthbert*, the prior of Lindisfarne, who died when Bede was fourteen.

Bede's own death at the age of 59 is told by another Cuthbert, one of Bede's disciples:

I can with truth declare that I never saw with my eyes or heard with my ears anyone return thanks so unceasingly to the living God ... Upon the floor of his cell singing 'Glory be to the Father and to the Son and to the Holy Ghost' and the rest, he peacefully breathed his last breath.

Bede was buried in St Paul's Monastery, now in Jarrow, in 735, but within a few centuries he became something of a movable priest. In 1022 his bones were taken to Durham and interred with those of St Cuthbert, then in 1370 they were rehoused in a shrine in the cathedral's Galilee Chapel. But this was not to be Bede's final resting place. When the shrine was destroyed in 1540, his remains were re-entombed on the same site, before being placed in their present location beneath polished limestone. This bears the inscription:

HAC SUNT IN FOSSA BEDAE VENERABILIS OSSA
(In this tomb are the bones of the Venerable Bede)

Legend has it that the term 'Venerable' was actually a divine gift to the scholar priest. A monk given the task of writing Bede's epitaph was unable to complete the line satisfactorily, leaving a gap between the words 'Bedae' and 'ossa'. When he returned to his work the next morning he discovered that the angels had filled the space with the word 'venerabilis'.

Today some of Bede's own words also appear above his tomb, in Latin and then in English:

Christ is the morning star
Who when the night
Of this world is past
Brings to his saints
The promise of
The light of life
& opens everlasting day ...

ABOVE St Paul's Monastery, home of the Venerable Bede. The Anglo-Saxon church partly survives as the chancel of the parish church; here the church tower is seen through the ruins of the monastic buildings.

Mount Grace Priory

The earliest known English autobiography is that of an illiterate woman from King's Lynn in Norfolk. *The Book of Margery Kempe*, begun in the 1430s, was dictated by its author and transcribed in 1450 by the priest whose name, Salthows, appears on the final page of the manuscript. Instead of using the first person, the subject of the memoir refers to herself throughout as 'this creature', and enlivens many of the incidents described with dialogue. On the book's first page are the words 'This boke is of Mountegrace', and annotations in the text – the comments and emendations of four of its earliest readers – name certain other monks who lived in the priory during the 15th century.

Margery Kempe married at twenty, and soon conceived her first child. But after the birth she 'went out of her mind and was amazingly disturbed and tormented with spirits', symptoms which would now be referred to as post-partum psychosis. Margery lived the life of a busy medieval woman: she went on to have another thirteen children and to set up a brewery, but after the failure of her business she felt called to lead a spiritual life, persuading her husband to join her in a vow of chastity. The worthy Kempe did his best, but the challenge was not an easy one:

> It happened one Friday, Midsummer Eve, in very hot weather – as this creature was coming from York carrying a bottle of beer in her hand, and her husband a cake tucked inside his clothes against his chest – that her husband asked his wife this question: 'Margery, if there came a man with a sword who would strike off my head unless I made love with you as I used to do before, tell me on your conscience – for you say you will not lie – whether you would allow my head to be cut off, or else allow me to make love with you again, as I did at one time?'
>
> 'Alas, sir,' she said, 'why are you raising this matter, when we have been chaste for these past eight weeks?'
>
> 'Because I want to know the truth of your heart.'
>
> And then she said with great sorrow, 'Truly, I would rather see you being killed, than that we should turn back to our uncleanness.'
>
> And he replied, 'You are no good wife.'

Finally, Kempe agreed to continue the vow if his wife paid his debts before embarking on her pilgrimage to Jerusalem.

Margery expressed her devotion with loud wailing and weeping, seeing the trials she endured at the hands of her detractors as sufferings for Jesus. The book describes her pilgrimages to the Holy Land, Italy and Spain, and the difficulties she experienced with her fellow pilgrims, who found her a trying companion.

ABOVE The Carthusian monastery at Mount Grace was built in the 14th century; the ruins are the best preserved of the ten Carthusian monasteries in Britain.

In 1491 a monk whose name appears on the 'Mountgrace' manuscript of Kempe's text completed the first translation into Latin of the English mystical work *The Cloud Of Unknowing*. Though Richard Methley lived and worked at Mount Grace in the 15th century, his translation is of a 14th-century text by an unknown author, probably a priest. *The Cloud of Unknowing* offers a spiritual path derived from the writings of a 6th-century Syrian monk, known as pseudo-Dionysius. This teaching embraces the *via negativa* – the idea of the utter unknowability of God – asserting that understanding comes not through the intellect but through love, and describing a path of contemplation and prayer.

Nicholas Love, prior at Mount Grace from 1416, also translated a key spiritual text of the period, but this time from Latin into English. *Meditationes Vitae Christi* was written by a 14th-century Franciscan but attributed to St Bonaventure, and Love's version, with some additions and deletions of his own, came into English as *The Mirror of the Blessed Life of Jesus Christ*. The work, translated into many European languages at that time, was intended for use during meditation, and is an imaginative account of Christ's life, focusing on his childhood and passion. Part of Love's manuscript is still in the possession of the priory.

It is interesting that in addition to its obvious Christian associations, Mount Grace Priory also has a link with the Moslem country of Iraq through the life and writings of Gertrude Bell. The Bell family were industrialists from the north of England, where they owned a number

RIGHT Gertrude Bell picnicking with King Faisal of Iraq in 1922; photograph from the second volume of her letters.

of estates in Northumberland and Durham, including that of Mount Grace. In a letter written to her father after a round-the-world trip in 1902, Gertrude recalls how 'that bit of country round Mount Grace is lovely – in all lights and seasons', and the following year she wrote from Japan that it would be 'nice to have a Japanese cherry grove', and she hoped to 'induce our respected father and grandfather to let us make a plantation at Rounton or Mount Grace'.

Gertrude was the first woman to achieve a first in Modern History at Oxford, and she learned Farsi and Arabic when still a young woman. Widely travelled and an intrepid mountaineer, she never married but fell passionately in love with a married major who was killed at Gallipoli. After his death she settled in Baghdad as the only female member of the British Expeditionary Force in Mesopotamia, becoming political adviser to King Faisal in the newly formed country of Iraq, which she had helped to found. Later, Gertrude founded the country's National Museum, of which she was director. She died of an overdose shortly before her 58th birthday, leaving hundreds of letters, sixteen diaries and thousands of photographs of her travels.

ABOVE The priory church seen from the south-east. The ruins are located in woodland, beneath the open spaces of the North York Moors.

Rievaulx Abbey, Byland Abbey and Fountains Abbey

Several unique texts by three very different writers were inspired by or written in these great Cistercian abbeys. In the mid-12th century, Aelred of Rievaulx, who became abbot there at the age of 37, wrote a series of works on the subject of love and friendship inspired by the Roman orator Cicero's *De Amicitia* ('On Friendship'). The first, *The Mirror of Love*, celebrates Aelred's own experience of love for a young monk whose death had caused him terrible grief:

> It was as if my body had been eviscerated and my helpless
> soul rent in pieces ...
> O wretched life, O grievous life, a life without Simon.

Aelred reassures his reader of the chastity of his feelings by referring to the 'disciple whom Jesus loved', explaining that spiritual love is a gift of God's grace. He uses the metaphor of the kiss to explain how two friends, kissing in spiritual friendship, not only unite their own hearts but begin a journey of union with Christ. However, he warns old monks who share a bed with young monks not to be complacent about the innocence of their feelings. Aelred himself experienced many intense spiritual friendships with young monks at the abbey.

In his *Mirror of Chastity*, Aelred describes spiritual love as a foretaste of heaven, again emphasising that chastity is the 'flower and adornment of all the virtues'.

Despite the fact that he was a cleric himself, and popular for his sermons at York Minster, for Laurence Sterne chastity was never a priority. He wrote the first two volumes of *Tristram Shandy* (1759–62) while his curate took over his parish duties, and he embarked on an affair with a singer just after they were published.

Sterne's book is an extraordinary parody of the novel, which at the time was a new literary form. Tristram's narrative is presented as an erratic stream of consciousness in disordered sequence and interrupted by frequent digressions. The book was not greatly liked by the literary establishment of the time, but it made Sterne famous and enabled him to take his wife and daughter to live in France and Italy for several years. On

LEFT A pattern of arches at Rievaulx, one of the most atmospheric of the country's ruined abbeys. Founded in 1131 and the first Cistercian abbey in the north, Rievaulx became one of the wealthiest monasteries of medieval England.

his return in 1767 he published two volumes of sermons, and fell in love with the young wife of an official in the East India Company. His *Journal to Eliza*, written when she left for India, was an uncharacteristically sentimental expression of his feelings. Here, he describes to her a place he often visited on an 'afternoon pilgrimage' – Byland Abbey:

> These remains are situated on the banks of a clear gliding stream; on the opposite side whereof rises a bold ridge of hills, thick with wood – and finely varied by jutting rocks and broken precipices; and these are so very abrupt, that they now not only by their magnitude, but by the shade they cast, increase the solemnity of the place. – Many parts of the ruin are still entire; the refectory is almost perfect, and a great part of the chapel.

Sterne died the following year. His corpse suffered the indignity of being stolen from its grave for use as a model in an anatomy lecture. However, it was recognised as the earthly remains of a well-known clergyman and novelist, and quietly replaced.

A Sheffield master-founder who became a best-selling political poet took time to appreciate the beauty of Fountains Abbey in his sonnet of that name:

> Abbey! for ever smiling pensively,
> How like a thing of nature dost thou rise
> Amid her loveliest works! as if the skies,
> Clouded with grief, were arched thy roof to be,
> And the tall trees were copied all from thee!

By contrast, the themes characteristic of the writing of Ebenezer Elliott were poverty and injustice, and his *Corn Law Rhymes* (1830), a series of poems condemning the Bread Tax, achieved immediate fame and popularity. But as he himself wrote,

> 'He who lives in a chimney will do well to take the air when he can, and ruralize now and then'.

ABOVE Fountains Abbey was founded as a Cistercian monastery in 1132. Both the architecture of the abbey and the landscape in which it stands, a World Heritage Site, are of outstanding historical and aesthetic importance.

Whitby Abbey

England's first great historical writer, the Venerable Bede, devotes an entire chapter of his Latin text, *The Ecclesiastical History of the English People* (731), to the 663 Synod of Whitby, an assembly at the abbey to agree, among other things, a method for fixing the date of Easter. The practice of the Celtic Christians differed from that appointed by the Roman Church – a cause of great and longstanding controversy – and the assembled monks and missionaries 'resolved to conform to that which they found to be better'. Not surprisingly, the outcome was a victory for Rome.

In the same text Bede mentions the first poet to compose in the Anglo-Saxon vernacular, Caedmon:

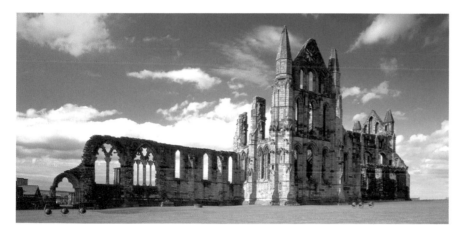

LEFT
Whitby Abbey was founded in 657 by Hild, later St Hilda, whose Christian example and reputation spread throughout England and beyond.

FAR LEFT
Silhouette of the north transept at sunset.

> In this monastery of Whitby there lived a brother whom God's grace made remarkable. So skilful was he in composing religious and devotional songs, that he could quickly turn whatever passages of Scripture that were explained to him into delightful and moving poetry in his own English tongue.

According to Bede, Caedmon, who had entered the monastery when already an old man, was an uneducated oxherd working on the lands of the abbess Hild. Bede tells how Caedmon received the gift of song in a dream, and went on to make many poems about the Creation, and early human history. The only piece that can be reliably attributed to him, however, is the nine-line *Hymn of Creation*, containing the lines:

> Then the Guardian of Mankind adorned
> this middle-earth below, the world for men ...

Hild, a relative of the Northumbrian king, founded the double house for nuns and monks at Streaneshalch, or Whitby, in 657, and was abbess until her death in 680. Renowned for her wisdom, she is frequently referred to in the second canto of Sir Walter Scott's narrative poem *Marmion* (1808). In this section of the poem a perjured nun, Constance of Beverley, in love with Lord Marmion, has received his love in return and followed him disguised as his page. However, Marmion deserts her for the wealthy Lady Clare, and the unfortunate Constance is brought before the current abbess, a woman whose aim is to 'emulate St Hilda's fame'. The abbess and some of her nuns sail from Whitby to Lindisfarne for the inquisition, at which Constance will learn her fate:

> It curl'd not Tweed alone, that breeze,
> For, far upon Northumbrian seas,
>   It freshly blew, and strong,
> Where, from high Whitby's cloister'd pile,
> Bound to St Cuthbert's Holy Isle
>   It bore a bark along.

Tragic love affairs are also the subject of *Sylvia's Lovers* (1863), a novel by Elizabeth Gaskell that was inspired by her visit to Whitby with two of her daughters in 1859. The Manchester-based writer had started visiting Yorkshire in 1855 when she was researching her biography of Charlotte Brontë, and the novel that grew from a fortnight's stay in Whitby focuses on the town's whaling tradition and memories of the activities of the press gangs during the French Revolutionary Wars. Gaskell renames the town Monkshaven, and the novel opens with a detailed description of the place and its history:

> Monkshaven was a name not unknown in the
> history of England, and traditions of its having been
> the landing-place of a throneless queen were
> current in the town. At that time there had been a
> fortified castle on the heights above it, the site of
> which was now occupied by a deserted manor-
> house; and at an even earlier date than the arrival
> of the queen, and coeval with the most ancient
> remains of the castle, a great monastery had stood
> on those cliffs, overlooking the vast ocean that
> blended with the distant sky.

Elizabeth Gaskell's novel explores how the private lives of her characters – Sylvia Robson, and the two men who love her – are touched by public events. Sylvia's suitor, bold Charley Kinraid, is seized by the press gang, but a message he sends to reassure her is concealed by her conventional cousin Philip, in the hope that she will marry him instead. This she does. But when after some years Charley returns and the deception is revealed to heartbroken Sylvia, a repentant Philip leaves and enlists. He returns a disfigured man, but dies, forgiven, in Sylvia's arms.

The fate of another fictional young woman is sealed within sight of Whitby Abbey in Bram Stoker's *Dracula* (1897): that of Lucy Westenra. Count Dracula is shipped from Varna to Whitby in one of fifty earth-filled boxes, and disembarks as a wolf, having despatched the entire ship's crew en route. Once on dry land, he proceeds to suck the blood of Lucy, best friend of Mina Murray, whose fiancé Jonathan Harker has already visited Dracula in his Transylvanian castle. Mina's journal innocently sets the scene in Whitby, its author little knowing that this will be the location of the horrific death of her friend:

> Right over the town is the ruin of Whitby Abbey ... It is a most noble ruin, of immense size, and full of beautiful and romantic bits; there is a legend that a white lady is seen in one of the windows. Between it and the town there is another church, the parish one, round which is a big graveyard, all full of tombstones. This is to my mind the nicest spot in Whitby, for it lies right over the town, and has a full view of the harbour and all up the bay to where the headland called Kettleness stretches out into the sea.

With Lucy no longer able to satisfy the count's gory appetites as she is now a vampire herself, Dracula turns his attentions to the hapless Mina. But the box containing the count is at length pursued to Transylvania, where beheading and a stab through the heart finally put paid to his nocturnal feasting, and Mina survives to marry Harker.

Stoker had left his job in the Irish civil service in 1878 to work at the Lyceum Theatre as secretary and touring manager to the flamboyant actor-manager Henry Irving, remaining in his employ for twenty-seven years. It is probable that Irving's magnetic personality and mannered speech and gait were the inspiration for Stoker's extraordinary count.

ABOVE The abbey's gaunt remains have inspired many writers, including Bram Stoker, the author of *Dracula*.

Scarborough Castle

In May 1849 Anne Brontë, weak with consumption, arrived in Scarborough. She had spent five lively summers there from 1840 to 1845 as governess to the children of the Reverend Edmund Robinson, enjoying the cultural life of the town if not her work with the family. The Robinsons always holidayed in style, renting a Georgian house overlooking South Bay with views across to the castle on the headland, and on this occasion Anne, her sister Charlotte and friend Ellen Nussey booked rooms in the same house: No. 2, The Cliff.

Anne may not have enjoyed educating the Robinsons' children, but this had been a good position for her, and she had happily proposed her brother Branwell as tutor to their son in 1842. The arrangement seemed to be working well; then suddenly, in 1845, Branwell was dismissed. His passionate affair with the invalid vicar's vivacious wife, Lydia, had been discovered. Anne's position was now impossible and she resigned, but the abrupt ending of the relationship set Branwell on a path of excessive drinking that irretrievably ruined his health and fortunes.

It was during the period following this scandal that Anne wrote her novels, and both *Agnes Grey* and *The Tenant of Wildfell Hall* reflect her experiences with the Robinsons, and the atmosphere of the Scarborough she knew. The second novel also clearly draws on the character of Branwell. The author was accused by one reviewer of having 'a morbid love for the coarse', and Charlotte commented that 'the choice of subject was an entire mistake', yet the novel was a popular success.

But 1848, the year of its publication, was overshadowed by the deaths of both Emily and Branwell from consumption. Anne already knew she had the disease, but in January of the following year, when a reputable physician told her she had only a few months to live, she expressed her anguish in poetry:

The Brontë sisters, painted by Patrick Branwell Brontë, circa 1834.

> A dreadful darkness closes in
> On my bewildered mind;
> O let me suffer and not sin,
> Be tortured yet resigned.
>
> Through all this world of whelming mist
> Still let me look to Thee,
> And give me courage to resist
> The Tempter till he flee …

Towards the end of March Anne expressed a wish to visit the seaside, but Charlotte was anxiously resistant to the idea, and even when the plan was agreed she kept delaying their departure. However, on 24 May they finally set out for Scarborough, visiting York Minster en route.

The day after their arrival Anne's condition worsened and she realised she was going to die, but there was not enough time to return home to Haworth. Ellen Nussey describes their last evening together in a letter to Elizabeth Gaskell:

> The evening closed in with the most glorious sunset ever witnessed. The castle on the cliff stood in proud glory gilded by the rays of the declining sun. The distant ships glittered like burnished gold; the little boats near the beach heaved on the ebbing tide, inviting occupants. The view was grand beyond description. Anne was drawn in her easy chair to the window, to enjoy the scene with us.

Anne died the following afternoon. She is buried in St Mary's churchyard, beneath the ruins of the castle.

ABOVE Built in the early 13th century on the site of an earlier fortification, Scarborough Castle dramatically dominates the headland and the town below.

Clifford's Tower

In 1190, 800 Jews took refuge in Clifford's Tower, then a wooden structure, after a mob had started to attack them in the streets of the town. They were given a choice: to be baptised as Christians, or be killed. In his poem *Astringencies* (1961), **Jon Silkin** tells how they refused both and instead:

> Took each other's lives
> To escape christian death
> By christian hand; and the last
> Took his own.

The tower was burned to the ground and rebuilt in stone, and Silkin remarks on the fact that there have been no synagogues in the town since this time:

> Absence of Jews
> Through hatred, or indifference,
> A gap they slip through, a conscience
> That corrodes more deeply since it is
> Forgotten – this deadens York.

For Silkin, this horrific 12th-century event has the 'frigid persistence of a growth', and he concludes by linking it with the horrors of the 20th century:

> All Europe is touched
> With some of frigid York
> As York is now by Europe.

*Jon Silkin,
photograph by Ruth Dupré, 1999.*

ABOVE Clifford's Tower was built in stone in the 13th century on the site of a motte-and-bailey castle with a timber keep, constructed in 1068 by William the Conqueror.

Middleham Castle

ABOVE **Middleham Castle, home of Richard III, was built in the 12th century on the site of a Norman motte-and-bailey castle.**

In 1462 a young man joined the household of his cousin, the Earl of Warwick, at Middleham Castle, to learn the skills and tactics of combat and to make his way in the world. Here he fell in love with Warwick's daughter, Anne, and the couple settled at Middleham after their marriage in 1472. From the castle he carried out his duties as Lord of the North with legendary fairness and diligence on behalf of his brother, the king, and when he became king himself in 1483 the people of Middleham rejoiced. But his short reign was full of personal tragedy – caused by the death of his young son and then of his wife – before he himself was cut down on the battlefield at the age of only 31. The young man was Richard of Gloucester, England's King Richard III.

If this is not our usual image of the last Plantagenet king, many would say it is because **William Shakespeare** took his poetic licence with the character to an unfair extreme. In the opening scene of *Richard III*, the future king introduces himself to the audience as:

> Cheated of feature by dissembling nature,
> Deform'd, unfinish'd, sent before my time
> Into this breathing world scarce half made up,
> And that so lamely and unfashionable
> That dogs bark at me as I halt by them.

Not only does Shakespeare make Richard a hunchback, he also portrays him as full of evil intent, seducing Anne for his own political ends and notoriously arranging the murder of the two young princes, his nephews, in the Tower.

If Shakespeare was Richard's principal character assassin, Horace Walpole was his chief advocate. When it appeared in 1768, Walpole's *Historic Doubts on the Life and Reign of King Richard the Third* was an immediate success. He was drawn to the subject by an enthusiasm for the truth, and an instinct that 'many of the crimes imputed to Richard seemed improbable; and, what was stronger, contrary to his interest'. His detailed and entertaining argument attempts to shift some of the blame for Richard's reputation on to Henry VII:

> Henry's character, as we have received it from his apologists, is so much worse and more hateful then Richard's, that we may well believe Henry invented and propagated by far the greater part of the slanders against Richard: that Henry, not Richard, probably put to death the true duke of York, as he did the earl of Warwick.

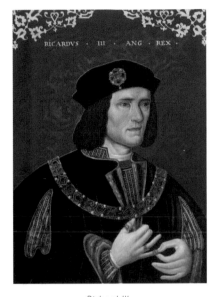

Richard III,
painting by an unknown artist,
late 15th or late 16th century.

According to Walpole, Richard was the victim of 15th-century political propaganda; 'suspicions and calumny were fastened on Richard' by the Lancastrian historians whose job was to make the 'mean and unfeeling tyrant' Henry VII appear noble and wise. Shakespeare subsequently adopted the same line in order to flatter his Tudor monarch, Henry's granddaughter Elizabeth I.

Walpole was himself no stranger to the world of politics. The youngest son of Prime Minister Robert Walpole, he served as an MP for twenty-five years, though he was more interested in sharing gossip than exercising power, and his *Letters*, written to a wide variety of friends, are uniquely revealing of the politics and society of the England of his time.

As well as tackling the political intrigues of which Richard is accused, Walpole turns a spotlight on the king's supposed deformity. After surveying some anecdotal evidence, he dismisses the image of a 'little, crooked, withered, hump-back'd monster' in favour of a figure that was slender and short but 'not well made about the shoulders'.

Thus Walpole's *Historic Doubts* casts the erstwhile resident of Middleham in a softer light; but neither this volume nor more recent fictional accounts, such as Sharon Penman's *The Sunne in Splendour* (1982), have managed to erase Shakespeare's indelible portrait.

Hardwick Old Hall and Hardwick Hall

'Solitary, poor, nasty, brutish and short': this was the view of human existence expressed by the philosopher Thomas Hobbes. Yet in his own long life he enjoyed the friendship and patronage of the Dukes of Devonshire, met Galileo in Italy, and reaped the rewards of his own extraordinary intellectual gifts. By the age of 14 he had translated Euripides' drama *Medea* from Greek into Latin verse, and in his late 80s he completed a translation of Homer's great epics, the *Iliad* and *Odyssey*.

Hobbes's philosophical text *Leviathan* (1651) adopts an uncompromisingly materialist view of the world and human nature, greatly influenced by the science of Galileo. We are sophisticated machines, Hobbes explains, but our animal nature puts us always at war with one another. If we are to enjoy any individual freedom under such circumstances, we need to enter into mutual agreement – a commonwealth or social contract. But this radical philosophy has a surprisingly conservative political solution for Hobbes: a system ruled by hereditary monarchy.

These royalist sympathies were not simply philosophical, however. In fear of his life, Hobbes had spent the years of Parliamentarian rule abroad, working as mathematics tutor to the future Charles II. It was Charles who later intervened when *Leviathan* was being examined for evidence of atheism in the witch-hunt that followed the Great Fire. The king saved its author, but forbade him to publish further philosophical works.

During the last few years of his life Hobbes lived with the Earl of Devonshire at Chatsworth and Hardwick Hall, translating Homer and completing his autobiography in both English prose and Latin verse. Hardwick Hall was built in the 1590s by the architect Robert Smythson for Bess of Hardwick, one of the most colourful women of Elizabethan England. Bess had been born at the manor house now known as Hardwick Old Hall, which she set about enlarging in the late 1580s after her separation from her husband, Lord Shrewsbury. Before this project was finished, and following her substantial inheritance at Shrewsbury's death, she commissioned Smythson to begin work on the magnificent new Hardwick Hall, a hundred yards from the Old Hall.

It was here, nearly a century later, that Hobbes was staying before he died. James Wheldon, Hobbes's executor, describes the philosopher's final days in a letter written in January 1679 to Hobbes's friend, the biographer and antiquary John Aubrey:

ABOVE Hardwick Old Hall
and the East Lodge viewed
from the roof of the New
Hall. Bess of Hardwick
abandoned renovation work
on the Old Hall when in
1591 she embarked on a
glamorous new house
immediately next to it.

My lord being about to remove from Chatsworth to Hardwick,
Mr Hobbes would not be left behind; and therefore was a feather
bed laid into the coach; upon which he lay warm clad, he was
conveyed safely, and was in appearance as well after that little
journey as before it. But seven or eight days after, his whole right
side was taken with the dead palsy, and at the same time he was
made speechless ... He seemed to die rather for want of the fuel
of life (which was spent in him) and mere weakness and decay,
than by power of his disease.

Hobbes died at Hardwick Hall and was buried in the church at Ault
Hucknall. His reputed last words, presumably uttered before the 'dead
palsy' curtailed his power of speech, reveal a mind unafraid of the
ultimate challenge despite a belief in the mortality of the soul:

I am about to take my last voyage, a great leap in the dark.

Peveril Castle

According to the opening of Sir Walter Scott's novel *Peveril of the Peak* (1823), William the Conqueror gave his illegitimate son 'a liberal grant of property and lordships in Derbyshire' soon after the Battle of Hastings. William did not see illegitimacy as 'any bar to the course of his royal favour' since he himself rejoiced in the title of 'Gulielmus Bastardus', and this gift of lands enabled his son, William Peveril, to build 'that Gothic fortress, which, hanging over the mouth of the Devil's Cavern, so well known to tourists, gives the name of Castleton to the adjacent village'.

Scott notes that Peveril 'chose his nest upon the principles on which an eagle selects her eyry, and built it in such a fashion as if he had intended it ... for the sole purpose of puzzling posterity'. The hero of his novel is not this particular Peveril, however, but one Sir Geoffrey Peveril, an old Cavalier, and 'the representative of this ancient family' in the time of Charles II. The story is set against the alleged Jesuit plan of 1678 to assassinate the king, the so-called Popish Plot, and it involves a secret love affair between Sir Geoffrey's son and the daughter of a Puritan neighbour. After a lengthy series of intrigues and machinations – Scott himself grew tired of the book 'most damnably' when writing it – Sir Geoffrey is released from imprisonment in the Tower, and consents to his son's marriage.

Peveril of the Peak was not rapturously received by the critics. Scott was accused of profanity and excessive padding (the book ran to four volumes), and the selling price of two guineas was considered excessive. But a bad press and commercial success were easy bedfellows even in 1823, and *Peveril of the Peak* was greatly enjoyed by Scott's readers including, in due course, one of his greatest admirers, Charlotte Brontë.

Charlotte made her own visit to Peveril Castle in 1845, during a holiday in the Peak District that was to be of great creative significance for her. Charlotte and her friend Ellen Nussey stayed for three weeks at the home of Ellen's brother Henry, who was curate at Hathersage. Henry Nussey had once proposed to Charlotte in the businesslike manner she was later to ascribe to St John Rivers when proposing to Jane Eyre, and the moorland around Hathersage is clearly reconstructed as the landscape of the novel. The planning for *Jane Eyre* was evidently uppermost in Charlotte's mind at this time.

Scott had been an enormous influence on Charlotte's juvenile writing, so she will have had a lively awareness of the literary significance

of Peveril Castle. She and Ellen had borrowed a pony for their visit to Castleton and the caverns, enabling them to ascend the steep slope to the castle. It seems from Ellen's letter to a friend that they were accompanied, at least for part of the visit, by some rather chatty young women, a situation clearly not appreciated by Charlotte since 'the mirth of the Miss Halls was rather displeasing to her'. Despite the fact that even in Scott's day the place was 'well known to tourists', Charlotte always preferred to enjoy the landscape in silence. Ten years later, when she married, she was to feel profoundly grateful to her husband for understanding this, and his loving solicitude gave her nine months of happiness before she died.

ABOVE Peveril Castle was founded soon after the Norman Conquest by William Peveril, one of King William's most trusted knights. The great square tower, built by Henry II in 1176, offers breathtaking views of the neighbouring peaks and the village of Castleton below.

Ashby de la Zouch Castle

Sir Walter Scott,
portrait by Sir Edwin Landseer, 1824.

When **Sir Walter Scott** announces in *Ivanhoe* (1819) that 'Prince John held his high festival in the Castle of Ashby', the reader is quickly disabused of the notion that it was 'the same building of which the stately ruins still interest the traveller'. The ruins with which Scott and subsequent visitors are familiar evolved from a 12th-century manor house, not achieving castle status until the 15th century.

Scott enjoys fleshing out the history of his fictional setting, telling us that the castle and town of Ashby belonged at that time to Roger de Quincy, whose absence at the Crusades gave Prince John the opportunity to occupy his castle and dispose of his 'domains'.

Whatever the facts may have been, Scott uses the 12th-century environs of Ashby with relish when he is setting the scene for the great tournament, where the heroic Saxon, Wilfred of Ivanhoe, and the dastardly Templar, Brian de Bois-Guilbert, are to meet in combat:

> The scene was singularly romantic. On the verge of a wood, which approached to within a mile of the town of Ashby, was an extensive meadow of the finest and most beautiful green turf, surrounded on one side by the forest, and fringed on the other by straggling oak trees ...
>
> The ground, as if fashioned on purpose for the martial display which was intended, sloped gradually down on all sides to a level bottom, which was inclosed for the lists with strong palisades ...
>
> On a platform beyond the southern entrance, formed by a natural elevation of the ground, were pitched five magnificent pavilions ...

Ivanhoe has returned from the Crusades eager to marry his sweetheart Rowena, despite having been disinherited by his disapproving father. He and King Richard, both in disguise, defeat all comers at the Ashby tournament, including the Templar, who has fallen in love with and seized the beautiful Jewess, Rebecca. Bois-Guilbert's passion for Rebecca and her resistance to his advances, as well as the more subterranean reciprocal passion between Ivanhoe and Rebecca, make thrilling reading. The Brontës and no doubt scores of lesser writers of romantic fiction were influenced by it.

Scott's account of the great tournament also includes a scene in which the legendary Robin Hood achieves the impossible by bettering the bullseye scored by an opponent in the archery competition:

And letting fly his arrow with a little more precaution than before, it lighted right upon that of his competitor, which it split into shivers ... 'This must be the devil, and no man of flesh and blood,' whispered the yeomen to each other; 'such archery was never seen since a bow was first bent in Britain.'

Scott's novel concludes more or less according to Oscar Wilde's formula: 'The good end happily, the bad unhappily: that's what fiction means.' *Ivanhoe* was a sensation, and inspired one of the earliest literary sequels: Thackeray's comic *Rebecca and Rowena*.

ABOVE The 15th-century castle at Ashby de la Zouch grew from a smaller manor house built in the 12th century. The photograph shows the tower, built in 1474 by Lord Hastings and blown in two during the Civil War.

Framlingham Castle

Henry Howard, Earl of Surrey, was the last man to be executed under Henry VIII. He was sentenced in 1547 to be hanged, drawn and quartered by a jury of his enemies; the charge: treasonable quartering of the royal arms with his own. In the event he was beheaded on Tower Hill. His remains, buried in Barking, were later re-interred in St Michael's, Framlingham.

Framlingham Castle was one of the Howard family homes, and Surrey spent much of his childhood here and at Kenninghall in Norfolk. Tutored in the classics and Italian literature, he took the opportunity offered by a spell in prison for a breach of the peace to develop his own literary gifts.

Surrey was a great literary innovator, though the formal revolution he instigated was not to reach its peak for another fifty years or more. He translated the *Aeneid* into unrhymed iambic pentameters, a form that came to be known as blank verse and was later adopted for dramatic purposes by William Shakespeare. Surrey also developed the Italian sonnet familiar to him from Petrarch, initiating a new structure for the fourteen lines that was also to be made famous by Shakespeare, with alternate rhymes and a concluding couplet:

RIGHT Framlingham Castle was built in the 12th century, on the site of an earlier castle, by the powerful Roger Bigod. With its lake, Framlingham Mere, it was designed both as a stronghold and a symbol of power and status.

Set me in earth, in heaven, or yet in hell,
In hill, in dale, or in the foaming flood;
Thrall, or at large, alive whereso I dwell,
Sick, or in health, in ill fame or in good.
Yours will I be, and with this only thought
Comfort myself when that my hope is nought.

Surrey was married at the age of 15 to Frances de Vere; however, his name became romantically linked with that of Elizabeth Fitzgerald, daughter of the Earl of Kildare, on the strength of just one sonnet in her praise which concluded with the lines:

> Beauty her mate, her virtues from above:
> Happy is he that may obtain her love.

Surrey was widely believed to be her lover, and the story of their supposed relationship was portrayed like that of Petrarch and Laura until disproven by scholars over four centuries later.

ABOVE The castle became the home of the Howard family, the Dukes of Norfolk. Henry Howard, Earl of Surrey, lived here as a child.

It was probably Surrey's haughty manner and quick temper, as much as his outspoken political ambition, that precipitated his downfall in the prime of life:

> Summer is come, for every spray now springs;
> The hart hath hung his old head on the pale;
> The buck in brake his winter coat he flings;
> The fishes float with new repaired scale …
>
> And thus I see among these pleasant things
> Each care decays, and yet my sorrow springs.

The two great poetic forms that Surrey introduced reached their zenith at the end of the century in which he lived, and are still part of the fabric of contemporary poetry.

Orford Castle

RIGHT Orford Castle: this polygonal keep was built between 1165 and 1173 by Henry II to help control the rebellious barons of Norfolk and Suffolk.

One day in the late 12th century the fishermen of Orford caught a strange creature in their nets: 'He was naked and was like a man in all his members, covered with hair and with a long shaggy beard.' So wrote the 13th-century abbot and chronicler Ralph of Coggeshall about the Orford merman. According to Ralph, the merman was taken to the castle and imprisoned there, but 'he would not talk, even when tortured and hung up by his feet'.

During the 20th century, Orford was at different times the site of a bombing range, a radar experimental laboratory and a test centre for nuclear bomb triggers. In the title poem of his collection *Salt Water* (1997), Poet Laureate Andrew Motion interleaves references to the military role of the village with the story of the merman, whose silence puzzles and angers the villagers:

They wound a rope around his net
and dragged him through the square,
up the looming castle keep,
then down the castle stair

and down and down and down and down
through wet-root-smelling air
into a room more cave than room
and hung him there.

The unfortunate merman is suspended by the tail and a fire is lit
beneath his head. But his persistent 'refusal' to speak unsettles the
villagers even more, and they finally release him:

They cut him down. They hauled him up
the whirlpool of the stair,
they dragged him past their wives and children
gawping in the square ...

Ralph of Coggeshall tells how the merman 'was allowed to go into the
sea, strongly guarded with three lines of nets, but he dived under the
nets'. In Motion's poem, the villagers carry him to the shore, and watch:

They slid him tail-first in the sea
and washed the bitter drops
of blood-crust from his finger ends
and salt-spit from his lips,

and all the while, still silently,
they watched the tide bring in
a brittle, dimpled, breaking flood
of silver through his skin,

then open up his glistening eyes
in which they saw their fear
rise up to greet them one last time
and fade, and disappear,

disappear while they stood back
like mourners in a grave,
and watched his life ebb out of theirs
wave by wave by wave.

Andrew Motion,
photograph by Steve Speller, 1992.

BELOW The 'whirlpool of
the stair': detail of the
staircase in the south turret.

Audley End

The palatial house and gardens at Audley End seem to have been on every 17th-century traveller's itinerary. John Evelyn, whose principal interest was gardening, visited in September 1654, and in his *Diary* (published posthumously in 1818) he describes the house as 'without comparison one of the statliest Palaces of the Kingdome'. Evelyn had travelled extensively on the Continent, studying Renaissance gardens and later advising his friend Charles II on horticultural design, but he is not without criticism of the grounds at Audley End:

> The Gardens are not in order, though well inclosed: It has also a
> Bowling ally, a nobly well walled, wooded and watred Park, full of
> fine collines and ponds, the river glides before the Palace, to
> which an avenue of lime-trees; but all this much diminished by its
> being placed in an obscure bottome.

Evelyn's *Diary* covers most of his life and is therefore much more comprehensive than that of his friend Samuel Pepys (written between 1660 and 1669), though because it was often written some time after the event it lacks the immediacy of Pepys's work. His influential work *Sylva or Discourse on Forest Trees* (1664) will have interested Pepys, who at this time held the post of clerk of the acts at the Navy Board, which advised estate owners to plant timber for the navy.

It is the cellars at Audley End that Pepys principally enjoys, and on his first visit in February 1660, he receives a very favourable impression of the house:

> The housekeeper shewed us all the house, in which the stateliness
> of the ceilings, chimney-pieces, and form of the whole was
> exceedingly worth seeing. He took us into the cellar, where we
> drank most admirable drink, a health to the King. Here I played
> my flageolette, there being an excellent echo. He shewed us
> excellent pictures; two especially, those of the four Evangelists
> and Henry VIII.

Wine, women and song were always Pepys's greatest pleasures. The presence of his wife on a subsequent trip in October 1667, however, will have impeded his usual pursuit of female company, though in the cellars he is able freely to indulge in the other two:

LEFT The 17th-century Audley End was built on a lavish scale by Thomas, Earl of Suffolk, in the hope that Queen Elizabeth would honour him with a visit. This ambition was not fulfilled, but the house became a royal residence when Charles II bought it in 1668.

*Samuel Pepys,
portrait by John Costerman, 1690s.*

> We went down and drank of much good liquor,
> and indeed the cellars are fine; and here my wife
> and I did sing to my great content.

But evidently something had put Pepys out of humour, as the house seems 'not so fine as it hath heretofore to me'. He is critical of the ceilings, the staircase, and the furniture and hangings, enjoying only the portrait 'of Harry the 8th done by Holben'.

Thirty years later, Audley End was the first major destination of the redoubtable Celia Fiennes on what she called her Northern Journey. In her preface to the *Journeys*, she notes that her travels 'were begun to regain my health by variety and change of aire and exercise' and she kept a diary 'that as my bodily health was promoted my mind should not appear totally unoccupied'. Celia's preoccupation with her health meant that she paid particular attention to spas, though she is as interested in mining and manufacturing as in the homes of the gentry. Perhaps it is her Roundhead ancestry that makes her careless of the specifics of aristocratic ownership; Audley End was commissioned by the first Earl of Suffolk:

> Thence we went to Audlyend a house of the
> Earle of Sussex which makes a noble appearance
> like a town, so many towers and buildings off
> stone within a parke which is walled round, a
> good River runs through it, we pass over the
> bridge; its built round 3 Courts, there are 30
> great and little towers on the top and a great
> Cupilow in the middle, the roomes are large and
> lofty with good old rich furniture ...

Unlike the accounts of Evelyn and Pepys, Celia's catalogue of parts appears to reserve judgement on the place. Her Puritan background might naturally incline her to regard such ostentation without enthusiasm, but it is as likely to be the outdated design that fails to impress. The often-prim Celia reserved her praise for the genuinely up to date.

Bury St Edmunds Abbey

One of the most prolific of English poets entered Bury St Edmunds Abbey as a young novitiate at the age of 15. John Lydgate was an admirer of Chaucer, 'Sithe off oure language he was the lodesterre', and he went on to become a court poet, writing enormously long works in Chaucerian 'high style'. His *Fall of Princes* (1438/9), which contains this line in praise of Chaucer, comprises some 26,000 lines, and his writing stamina evidently increased with age, as his works get progressively longer.

It is ironic that a master of such Herculean verbosity should state, in his *Secrets of Philosophers* (his last work, completed by a disciple after his death), that 'Woord is but wynd; leff woord and tak the dede', but he was writing to order for a series of powerful patrons who presumably felt that size was important, and many of these vast works were in fact translations from French and Latin originals.

Lydgate's shorter and better poems were written simply for himself, and he had many admirers and imitators, enjoying a reputation as lofty as Chaucer's until the 17th century. But despite some more recent attempts to revive his reputation, with 100,000 surviving lines of poetry to his name Lydgate is a more likely candidate for the Guinness Book of Records than any contemporary anthology.

Celia Fiennes visited Bury during her 'Great Journey' of 1698, recording her impressions of the abbey in her *Journal* (compiled in 1702):

> ... there are many Descenters in the town 4 Meeteing places with the Quakers and Anabaptiss, there is only the ruines of the Abby walls and the fine gate at the entrance that remaines stone well carv'd; it seemes to be a thriveing industrious town 4 gates in it.

The daughter of a Cromwellian colonel and a nonconformist herself in matters of spelling and grammar as well as of religion, Celia Fiennes regularly remarks on the number of 'Descenters' in the places she visits. Between 1685 and 1710 she travelled on horseback through every county in England during her 'tours', usually accompanied by a servant though occasionally alone, risking the attentions of highwaymen and the perils of 18th-century road surfaces.

An account of the abbey is also given by Daniel Defoe, another dissenter and great traveller, in his *A Tour Thro' the Whole Island of Great Britain*. Defoe published his travel experiences in 1724, five years after the appearance of his first novel, *Robinson Crusoe*. The son of a butcher, Defoe became a secret agent after several other ventures failed, travelling round the country for over a decade to gather information for his employer, a Tory politician. It was these journeys that formed the basis of his travel memoir.

Defoe writes appreciatively of the monks who founded the abbey:

> ... who chose so beautiful a situation for the seat of their
> retirement; and who built here the greatest and, in its time,
> the most flourishing monastery in all these parts of England.

But he is more cynical about their motives in having the remains of St Edmund brought here to be re-interred, noting that the resulting revenues from visiting pilgrims greatly increased the abbey's wealth. He concludes:

> The abbey is demolished; its ruins are all that is to be
> seen of its glory: out of the old building, two very
> beautiful churches are built ...

ABOVE The abbey at Bury St Edmunds: the west front and Samson's Tower. The building of this Benedictine abbey spanned the 11th and 12th centuries.

Defoe had been arrested and pilloried for an ironic pamphlet about the dissenters, and a century later William Cobbett was also to discover that the writing of pamphlets could be a risky business. Cobbett, who had been a successful farmer in Hampshire and Surrey, included an account of a visit to Bury in his collection of essays *Rural Rides* (1830). His agricultural background meant that he appreciated the qualities of the local terrain as well as of the local women:

> The land all along, to Bury St Edmund's is very fine; but no trees worth looking at. Bury, formerly the seat of an Abbot, the last of whom, was, I think, hanged, or somehow put to death, by that matchless tyrant, Henry VIII, is a very pretty place; extremely clean and neat: no ragged or dirty people to be seen, and women (young ones I mean) very pretty and very neatly dressed.

RIGHT The remains of the crypt of the abbey church.

Cobbett's contempt for the clergy and his political radicalism both surface humorously here, but he is never less than enthusiastic about Bury and its abbey:

> It has the remains of the famous abbey walls and the abbey gate entire; and it is so clean and so neat ... a famous spot in ancient times; greatly endowed with monasteries and hospitals. Besides the famous Benedictine Abbey, there was once a college and a friary; and as to the abbey itself, it was one of the greatest in the kingdom ...

Cobbett's life had been extraordinary by any standards. He was completely self-educated, had served as a soldier in America from 1784 to 1791, and then spent eight years in Philadelphia, where he became involved in political publishing. He returned to England because he had been convicted of libelling George Washington's physician, but he ended up doing two years in prison anyway when he published a pamphlet against the practice of flogging in the army.

In 1821 Cobbett disagreed with proposals put forward to alleviate rural poverty, and set out on horseback to see the situation for himself. His sometimes arrogant, often opinionated, always entertaining *Rural Rides* was the result.

Houghton House

Houghton House is reputed to be the Palace or House Beautiful of **John Bunyan**'s *Pilgrim's Progress*. Bunyan was born in 1628 at Elstow, near Bedford, and as he used many real Bedfordshire locations in the book, the connection is a likely one.

Bunyan was an itinerant tinker who became famous as a Nonconformist preacher during the Protectorate of Oliver Cromwell. However, after the Restoration he was arrested in a private house for preaching without a licence, refusing to escape even though forewarned by friends. The justice before whom he appeared was seemingly keen to release him, but Bunyan refused to stop his preaching, and spent most of the next twelve years in Bedford county jail.

Prisons were grim places in the 17th century, but Bunyan received reasonable treatment at the hands of his gaolers, even managing to preach to the other dissenters among his fellow prisoners. He also wrote several books during this time, and began work on his masterpiece, the prose allegory *The Pilgrim's Progress* (1678).

Bunyan's text is presented as the author's dream, in which he sees Christian fleeing the City of Destruction and journeying through the Slough of Despond, finding temporary refuge at House Beautiful:

> Then said *Christian* to the *Porter*, Sir, What house is this? and may I lodge here to night? The Porter answered, This House was built by the Lord of the Hill, and he built it for the relief and security of Pilgrims.

The Porter introduces Christian to 'one of the Virgins of this place ... a grave and beautiful Damsel, named *Discretion*':

> So she ran to the door, and called out *Prudence*, *Piety* and *Charity*, who after a little more discourse with him, had him in to the Family; and many of them meeting him at the threshold of the house, said, Come in thou blessed of the Lord; this House was built by the Lord of the Hill, on purpose to entertain such pilgrims in.

After a brief respite here, Christian visits many significant places including the Valley of the Shadow of Death, Vanity Fair, and the country of Beulah, before reaching the Celestial City. Bunyan's tale is made more

ABOVE The 17th-century mansion Houghton House, believed to be the inspiration for the Palace Beautiful in John Bunyan's *Pilgrim's Progress*.

interesting by the variety of people his hero encounters, from Mr Worldly Wiseman to Giant Despair, each representing a particular type or attitude. Bunyan gives to each an individuality of speech and manner that makes them more than mere allegorical figures, a deployment of caricature that was to be supremely developed by Dickens.

In the centuries since its publication, *The Pilgrim's Progress* has enjoyed an extraordinary popularity, second only to that of the Bible, and over 170 versions exist in translation.

'Discretion, Prudence, Piety and Charity welcoming Christian to the Palace Beautiful', by an unknown artist.

Wrest Park

RIGHT The fine gardens at Wrest Park, inspired by those at Versailles in Paris, are home to a large collection of stone and lead statues.

FAR RIGHT The park comprises a mix of formal gardens, open spaces and sheltered woodland.

Charles II was so delighted with a poem written by a former employee at Wrest Park that he offered him a handsome annual pension. At the age of 17, farmer's son Samuel Butler had moved from his native Worcestershire to a post in the household of the Countess of Kent. Here, he made the most of the access he was given to the family's extensive library and he met John Selden, the legal historian for whom he later worked as secretary.

Butler's long burlesque poem *Hudibras*, loosely based on the tale of Don Quixote, was published in three parts over two decades, the last part in 1677, when Butler was in his sixties. It introduces the reader to its eponymous hero in the energetic octosyllabic rhyming couplets that Butler sustains throughout, a style now referred to as 'Hudibrastic':

> Sir Hudibras his passing worth,
> The manner how he sallied forth;
> His arms and equipage are shown;
> His horse's virtues, and his own.
> Th' adventure of the bear and fiddle
> Is sung, but breaks off in the middle.

In fact, this breaking off in the middle turns out to be the whole point of the poem, with Butler's long topical digressions on the hot issues of the day – Civil War politics, hermetic philosophy, the nature of marriage – balancing the extraordinary misadventures of Sir Hudibras and his squire, Ralpho.

This mock-heroic tale of a Cromwellian colonel is told from the viewpoint of a confirmed Royalist and Anglican. This partly explains the monarch's enthusiasm, but the reading populace was equally enthusiastic and the work was a bestseller – the most popular poem of its day. Its mockery of Puritanism, and the liberties Butler takes with his rhymes, were a winning formula:

> When Gospel-Trumpeter, surrounded
> With long-ear'd rout, to battle sounded,
> And pulpit, drum ecclesiastick,
> Was beat with fist, instead of a stick;
> Then did Sir Knight abandon dwelling,
> And out he rode a colonelling.

During the course of the tale, Sir Hudibras endures imprisonment in the stocks and a cudgelling in his attempt to win the hand of a wealthy widow. Butler himself had married a woman of means, though the money was soon lost through unwise investments, and despite his extraordinary literary success, Butler died in poverty. The £100 annuity from the king, promised in a moment of enthusiasm, seems never to have been paid.

Waltham Abbey

When his dearest friend died at the age of 22, Alfred Tennyson spent the next seventeen years composing his elegy. Tennyson had met Arthur Hallam as a student at Cambridge, where the two shared an interest in poetry and philosophy, and in 1832 they set off together to Spain to join a revolutionary army. But Hallam died the following year in Vienna, and Tennyson vowed not to publish anything for ten years as a tribute to his friend. Instead, he embarked on *In Memoriam*, a series of poems that was finally published in 1850. This was to be a landmark year for Tennyson: he married Emily Sellwood after an engagement of fourteen years, and succeeded Wordsworth as Poet Laureate.

One of the most memorable passages of the poem, from canto 106, was inspired by the bells of Waltham Abbey ringing in the New Year (Tennyson had lived at nearby High Beech for several years from 1837):

Alfred Tennyson,
first Baron Tennyson,
by Samuel Laurence,
circa 1840.

> Ring out, wild bells, to the wild sky,   Ring out the old, ring in the new,
> The flying cloud, the frosty light: Ring, happy bells, across the snow:
> The year is dying in the night;   The year is going, let him go:
> Ring out, wild bells, and let him die.   Ring out the false, ring in the true.

As well as being an elegy, *In Memoriam* was regarded by Tennyson's contemporaries as a poem of hope, although to T S Eliot it expressed 'despair of a religious kind':

> Ring out the shapes of foul disease;
> Ring out the narrowing lust of gold;
> Ring out the thousand wars of old,
> Ring in the thousand years of peace.
>
> Ring in the valiant man and free,
> The larger heart, the kindlier hand;
> Ring out the darkness of the land;
> Ring in the Christ that is to be.

LEFT **The abbey gatehouse and bridge at Waltham Abbey were built in the late 14th century.**

In 1853 the Tennysons settled on the Isle of Wight, and their first son was born. It was twenty years since the loss of his friend, but Tennyson never forgot him. He named his son Hallam.

Kensal Green Cemetery

Many writers have their names written in stone on monuments at this Victorian city cemetery; there are biographers, travel and legal writers, playwrights and poets, and writers on religion, science and sport. Among them reputations wax and wane, but one whose influence on English letters has been profound is Leigh Hunt. Hunt was a poet in his own right, and one of his lines – 'Write me as one who loves his fellow men' – became his epitaph. But it is as the publisher and supporter of the Romantic poets, notably Keats and Shelley, that Hunt is chiefly remembered. Hunt was an ally of Keats when he was attacked as a 'cockney poet', and in 1822 he was present on the beach in Italy when Shelley's drowned body was cremated. A person of an amiable and optimistic disposition, he became the model for the character of Skimpole in Dickens's *Bleak House*.

RIGHT The cemetery at Kensal Green was established in 1832, the first of a number of large burial grounds on the outskirts of London. Plots here could be privately purchased in anticipation of better conditions than those in the city's municipal graveyards. The white memorial in the photograph is that of Leigh Hunt.

A poet of a very different order, Reverend Richard Barham, is also buried at Kensal Green. Barham's comic verse narratives, *The Ingoldsby Legends* (1837), were popular well into the 20th century, and 'The Jackdaw of Rheims', probably the most well known, was learned and recited by several generations of schoolchildren. Barham himself had become a priest in his mid-twenties after an early life of unusual high spirits, and he took up writing a decade later. Such was the popularity of *Ingoldsby* that by the turn of the century more than half a million copies had been sold.

Barham's legends draw on folktales of violence and the supernatural, an area that also interested novelist Wilkie Collins. A friend and sometime collaborator of Dickens, Collins was often accused of sensationalism, and his best-known works, *The Moonstone* and *The Woman in White*, are both intricate tales of crime and violence. Interred with Collins are the remains of Caroline Graves, the widow with whom he lived openly, though he was simultaneously involved with another woman, the mother of his three children, Martha Rudd.

In a grave maintained by the Dickens Fellowship lies Mary Hogarth, sister-in-law of Charles Dickens. Dickens married Catherine Hogarth in 1836, shortly after the publication of the first instalment of *The Pickwick Papers*, and in January of the following year the first of their ten children was born. Catherine's sister Mary joined the household, but one evening after a visit to the theatre she became suddenly ill, and died in Dickens's arms. He wore the ring which he then took from her finger for the rest of his life.

ABOVE The grey stone cross on its stepped plinth marks the grave of Wilkie Collins.

Such was his grief that Dickens was unable to complete his instalment of *The Pickwick Papers* in time for that month's deadline, but he did write Mary's epitaph: 'Young, beautiful, and good, God numbered her among his angels at the early age of seventeen.' Mary also became the model for Little Nell in *The Old Curiosity Shop*, which Dickens began to publish three years later. As Nell lies dying, the schoolmaster says: 'There is not an angel added to the Host of Heaven but does its blessed work in those that loved it here.' But Dickens was inconsolable, and for a time expressed a wish to be interred in her grave, though in the event this place was taken by Mary's father, George.

It is from the novels of Dickens that our picture of the horrors of Victorian London mostly derives, but the man whose journalism allowed the London poor to speak for themselves was Henry Mayhew. A dramatist as well as a journalist, Mayhew was co-founder in 1841 and joint editor of the comic – and initially radical – magazine *Punch*. Towards the end of that decade he began to write a series of articles in the *Morning Chronicle*, detailing the everyday sufferings of the poor of the capital, later turning his attention to prisons and the plight of children. His pieces often used the actual words of the people he had spoken to, and their impact on his readers undoubtedly paved the way for social reform.

Another *Morning Chronicle* contributor was William Makepeace Thackeray. Thackeray had begun his journalistic career in 1833 as proprietor of the weekly *National Standard*, which went out of publication soon afterwards, but he managed to make a living from journalism and short fiction. His wife Isabella suffered a mental breakdown after the birth of their third child, Harriet, in 1840; with Isabella in a private home and their children being reared by his mother in Paris, Thackeray wrote prolifically, contributing to *Punch* and publishing the first monthly instalments of *Vanity Fair* in 1847. It seems clear that Thackeray's excessive eating and drinking contributed to his relatively early death. His mother lies interred with him, and his daughter Harriet, the first wife of Virginia Woolf's father Leslie Stephen, is also buried in the cemetery.

A great admirer of Thackeray, Anthony Trollope began his work as a novelist from a very different background, his family having fled to the Continent to escape his father's debts. His mother had helped to alleviate the family's poverty through her own writing, and in 1834 was instrumental in the young Trollope's appointment to work as a civil servant at the Post Office (where he was responsible for introducing the pillar box to Britain). Alongside this career Trollope began to write novels, the fourth of which, *The Warden* (1855), initiated the Barsetshire series, for which he is best known. In fact, Trollope introduced the novel sequence to English fiction, with characters reappearing to connect the various plots. The Palliser novels formed another series, though he also wrote many individual works, and for a man with a full-time occupation his total achievement of forty-seven published novels – as well as an autobiography and many short stories – is astonishing.

The mother of Oscar Wilde lies in a common grave in the cemetery, though her wish was always to be buried on some wild coast or at sea. Lady Jane Wilde wrote patriotic poetry under the pen-name 'Speranza', and was known as a literary hostess in Dublin. She died in 1896, the year after publication of her son's greatest success, *The Importance of Being Earnest*, and also his greatest disaster, imprisonment with hard labour for homosexual offences. Oscar only survived her by four years, dying in Paris in 1900.

An English playwright whose sexuality attracted less attention during his lifetime is buried at Kensal Green. Terence Rattigan had his first West End success in his early twenties with a comedy, but he went on to write serious dramas with a strong moral focus, notably *The Winslow Boy* (1946), *The Deep Blue Sea* (1954) and *Separate Tables* (1956). His 1960 play *Ross* is based on an incident in the life of T E Lawrence. Although accused of being 'middle-brow', and falling from favour during the drama revolution of the 1960s, his plays are still performed and enjoyed. Rattigan died in Bermuda, and his remains were laid in the family grave at Kensal Green, though his name is not written on the memorial.

ABOVE The Dissenters' Chapel, completed in 1834, was designed by John Griffith of Finsbury in the Greek Revival style. Recently restored, it is now used for meetings and as a visitor centre.

Apsley House and Wellington Arch

Apsley House became the London home of Arthur Wellesley, first Duke of Wellington, after he returned from Waterloo in 1815. As the man who had defeated Napoleon, Wellington was the nation's hero, and according to an extraordinary first-hand account of the duke soon after the decisive battle, he was not shy of publicity.

Along with many relatives of the combatants and other interested parties, Thomas Creevey, the Whig MP and noted diarist, was staying in Brussels with his wife and daughters as the battle was being fought just twelve miles away. Upon hearing that the duke had returned from the battlefield, he decided to walk to his residence in the hope of catching a glimpse of him:

> As I approached, I saw people collected in the street about the house; and when I got amongst them, the first thing I saw was the Duke upstairs alone at his window. Upon recognising me, he immediately beckoned me with his finger to come up … The first thing I did, of course, was to put out my hand and congratulate him upon his victory. He made a variety of observations in his short, natural, blunt way, but with the greatest gravity all the time, and without the least approach to anything like triumph or joy. –'It has been a damned serious business,' he said.

Creevey's good fortune in being summoned to this special interview may seem fanciful, but it was corroborated in a later conversation by Wellington himself. The MP was privileged to hear the duke's account of the battle from his own lips:

> 'Blucher and I have lost 30,000 men. It has been a damned nice* thing – the nearest run thing you ever saw in your life. Blucher lost 14,000 on Friday night, and got so damnably licked I could not find him on Saturday morning.'
>
> *Wellington was using the word* nice *in the now obsolete sense 'Critical, doubtful; full of risk or uncertainty'.*

Aware of his amazing scoop, Creevey 'instantly went home and wrote to England by the same courier who carried his [the Duke's] dispatch'.

This interview after Waterloo is a highlight in the various journal extracts and letters that were collected together and published in 1903 as *The Creevey Papers*. Most of Creevey's letters were to his daughter-in-law and confidante Elizabeth Ord, and his racy and often indiscreet gossip is full of lively observations about many of the most prominent people of the age.

Creevey seems to have been a remarkable individual in his own right. After the death of his wife he became impoverished, but as fellow diarist Charles Greville records, he never gave way to self-pity or despair:

> He has no servant, no home, no creditors; he buys
> everything as he wants it at the place he is at; he has no ties
> upon him, and has his time entirely at his own disposal and
> that of his friends. He is certainly a living proof that a man
> may be perfectly happy and exceedingly poor ...

ABOVE Designed and built in the 1770s for Baron Apsley by the neoclassical architect Robert Adam, Apsley House became the home of the Duke of Wellington in 1817.

The Duke of Wellington was the childhood hero and early literary inspiration for Charlotte Brontë. In 1826, her father Patrick bought some toy soldiers for Branwell, Charlotte's brother, and the children adopted one each. Charlotte named hers the Duke of Wellington, and as a fictional character he features in the plays and stories of Angria, the imaginary country she created with her brother. In Charlotte's imagination, the duke lives not in a neoclassical house, but in a marble palace in a Saharan oasis:

> In the midst of an immense hall surrounded by pillars of fine &
> brilliant diamond the pavement sparkles with amethyst jasper &
> sapphire a large & cloudlike canopy hangs over the heads of the geni
> all studded with bright rubies from which a red clear light streams
> irradiating all around with its burning glow …

Charlotte's fascination with the duke did not wane in her maturity; in an essay entitled 'The death of Napoleon' (1843), written for Monsieur Heger, the teacher she fell in love with in Brussels, she compares the two great campaigners – to Wellington's advantage:

> Public opinion had great value for Napoleon, for Wellington public
> opinion is an idea, a nonentity which the breath of his powerful will
> can make disappear, like a soap bubble. Napoleon flattered the
> people and sought their applause; Wellington spurns it; if his own
> conscience approves, that is enough, all other praise irritates him …

After a lifetime in which, in her imagination, Wellington had reigned supreme as a fictional entity, Charlotte did at last get to see her hero in the flesh. In 1850, on one of her infrequent visits to London, her publisher and friend George Smith took her to the Chapel Royal to catch a glimpse of the 80-year-old Wellington, and they followed him back to Apsley House. After so much eloquence about the imaginary duke, all Charlotte could find to say when she finally saw him was, 'He is a real grand old man'.

When Wellington died in 1852, Alfred, Lord Tennyson was already Poet Laureate, with some of his greatest works, including *In Memoriam* and *The Lotus-Eaters*, already published. As laureate, it was appropriate that he should commemorate the passing of England's great statesman and soldier, and his *Ode on the Death of the Duke of Wellington* was written in the sonorous Pindaric style:

Bury the Great Duke
With an Empire's lamentation,
Let us bury the Great Duke
To the noise of the mourning of a mighty nation,
Mourning when their leaders fall
Warriors carry the warrior's pall,
And sorrow darkens hamlet and hall ...

Lead out the pageant: sad and slow,
As fits an universal woe,
Let the long long procession go,
And let the sorrowing crowd about it grow,
And let the mournful martial music blow;
The last great Englishman is low.

Two years after his elegy to the man who had won a great military
victory, Tennyson wrote his most quoted poem, about a military
disaster. *The Charge of the Light Brigade* was published in December
1854, only weeks after the ill-fated cavalry charge at Balaclava during
the Crimean War, when due to an error hundreds of men on horseback
charged into the Russian cannons:

'Forward, the Light Brigade!'
Was there a man dismayed?
Not though the soldier knew
Someone had blundered:
Their's not to make reply,
Their's not to reason why,
Their's but to do and die:
Into the valley of Death
Rode the six hundred.

The line 'Someone had blundered' was omitted from the version of the
poem that appeared in his *Maud and Other Poems* collection in 1855,
but was subsequently acknowledged as the truth, and reinstated.

Thomas Hardy was a novelist in the 19th century and a poet in the
20th, but he also wrote a play that, although he had intended it for
'mental performance' only, was highly praised when scenes from it were
performed in London in 1914. *The Dynasts* is a huge work that had
occupied Hardy's thoughts for over thirty years before it began to appear

in 1904. Its subtitle, *An Epic Drama of the War with Napoleon in Three parts, Nineteen Acts and One Hundred and Thirty Scenes*, gives a clear indication of the extent and scope of the work, which opens in 1805 with Napoleon's threat of invasion and concludes ten years later with Waterloo. Towards the end of the play Hardy has the Duke of Wellington speak lines that are reminiscent of the report given to Creevey:

> From the intelligence that Gordon brings
> 'Tis pretty clear old Blucher had to take
> A damned good drubbing yesterday at Ligny,
> And has been bent hard back! So that, for us,
> Bound to the plighted plan, there is no choice
> But to do like … No doubt they'll say at home
> That we've been well thrashed too. It can't be helped …

Hardy's focus is not Wellington, however, but Napoleon, who he presents as a tragic figure, and the play also explores the effects of these great historical events on ordinary folk such as soldiers and Wessex rustics. Above them all, abstract 'Intelligences' comment on the action, as here in the 'Chorus of the Years':

> The snail draws in at the terrible tread,
> But in vain; he is crushed by the felloe-rim;
> The worm asks what can be overhead,
>
> And wriggles deep from a scene so grim,
> And guesses him safe; for he does not know
> What a foul red flood will be soaking him!
>
> Beaten about by the heel and toe
> Are butterflies, sick of the day's long rheum,
> To die of worse than the weather-foe.
>
> Trodden and bruised to a miry tomb
> Are ears that have greened but will never be gold,
> And flowers in the bud that will never bloom.

Hardy's play, though rich in poetry and dramatic originality, has suffered a fate similar to that of the statue of Wellington on horseback that originally crowned the Wellington Arch. Due to their vast dimensions, both have been consigned to obscurity.

Marble Hill House and Chiswick House

When George II gave Henrietta Howard the wherewithal to build a residence on the banks of the Thames in 1724, he was not only sponsoring a classic Palladian villa but also cementing a literary coterie. Henrietta was married to the Earl of Suffolk's youngest son and held a position as woman of the bedchamber to George's wife, Queen Caroline. She was also, with Caroline's full knowledge and approval, the king's mistress.

Alexander Pope, who lived nearby in Twickenham, took a great interest in the project, and the earliest known design for Marble Hill Park is attributed to him. In the event, he collaborated with Charles Bridgeman, the royal gardener, on the layout of the gardens, even requesting from his friend Lord Bathurst the loan of some sheep to keep the 'new springing grass' well trimmed. Pope, who had worked for many years on his own more modest house and garden, was renowned for having created a large grotto decorated with stones, shells and mirrors, and he gave special advice to Henrietta Howard on this particular feature of the park.

Pope and his friends the satirist Jonathan Swift and poet John Gay were frequent guests of Henrietta in the mid-1720s, when the house and gardens at Marble Hill were being established. Known as the three Yahoos of Twickenham after characters in Swift's satire *Gulliver's Travels* (1726), the friends were not above mocking each other, as here in Swift's poetic teasing of Pope's frequent supervisions of Moody, the Marble Hill gardener:

> Him twice a Week I here expect
> To rattle Moody for Neglect;
> An idle Rogue, who spends his Quartridge
> In tipling at the Dog and Partridge.

For wielding an even sharper pen, Pope had earned himself the sobriquet 'the wasp of Twickenham'; his poem *The Dunciad* (1743), a satire against 'Dulness', ridiculed many of the notable figures of the age, his friends among them. He certainly thought Henrietta Howard 'a reasonable woman, handsome and witty', but in *To a Lady* (1735) he has some less flattering things to say about his friend, referred to in the poem as Cloe:

She speaks, behaves, and acts just as she ought;
But never, never, reach'd one gen'rous Thought.
Virtue she finds too painful an endeavour,
Content to dwell in Decencies for ever.
So very reasonable, so unmov'd,
As never yet to love, or to be lov'd.
She, while her Lover pants upon her breast,
Can mark the figures on an Indian chest;
And when she sees her Friend in deep despair,
Observes how much a Chintz exceeds Mohair.
Forbid it Heav'n, a Favour or a Debt
She e'er should cancel—-but she may forget.

BELOW George II financed the building of this fine Palladian villa for his mistress, Henrietta Howard. Marble Hill is the last complete surviving example of the elegant villas which bordered the Thames between Richmond and Hampton Court in the 18th century.

In contrast to his fellow Yahoos, Gay was reputed to be a genial man. During the period of the building of Marble Hill he was working on the ballad opera that was to make his fortune (and that was based on an idea of Swift's), *The Beggar's Opera* (1728). His epitaph, beneath which he lies in Westminster Abbey, certainly testifies to a person of great good humour:

> Life is a jest, and all things show it;
> I thought so once, and now I know it.

Pope became a less frequent visitor to Marble Hill towards the end of his life. The explanation for this may lie in a letter he wrote in 1739 to one of his many correspondents, Lord Bathurst:

> A new Building is like a new Church, when once it is set up, you
> must maintain it in all the forms, and with all the inconveniences;
> then cease the pleasant luminous days of inspiration, and there's
> an end of miracles at once!

ABOVE Looking up to the classical portico at Chiswick House.

After Pope's death Horace Walpole became a regular visitor to Marble Hill. He had moved in 1747 into a cottage in Twickenham, where he spent a great deal of his time and attention – as Pope did at Marble Hill – extending and refurbishing the house and laying out the gardens at what was to become his 'little gothic castle' at Strawberry Hill. Walpole wanted to create a Gothic house to contrast with the Classical style that was predominant in Twickenham and Richmond, and his interest in the Gothic eventually resulted in a new literary genre, the Gothic novel, of which his *Castle of Otranto* was the first exponent.

Walpole used papier mâché for the fan vaulting of the long gallery at Strawberry Hill, and, following his advice, in 1755 Henrietta Howard created a new dining room at Marble Hill lined with Chinese paper. Three years later, at Walpole's instigation, she built a Gothic barn, the 'Priory of St Hubert'.

The man whom Walpole called the Apollo of the Arts, the third Earl of Burlington, had also received advice from Alexander Pope. Pope had been a regular dining companion of the Earl, Richard Boyle, and he helped William Kent design the informal layout of the gardens at Burlington's Chiswick House. It is in his famous verse *Epistle to Burlington* (1731) that Pope sets out his horticultural manifesto:

To build, to plant, whatever you intend,
To rear the Column, or the Arch to bend,
To swell the Terras, or to sink the Grot;
In all, let Nature never be forgot ...

Above all, Pope exhorts his correspondent to 'Consult the Genius of the Place in all', a motto for his own creative gardening at home in Twickenham. Writing to his intimate friends Teresa and Martha Blount, he describes, albeit with irony, the feeling he has for the garden he has created:

It is the place that of all others I fancy, and I am not yet out of humour with it ... It does not cease to be agreeable to me so late in the Season; the very dying of the leaves adds a variety of colours that is not unpleasant. I look upon it as upon a Beauty I once loved, whom I should preserve a respect for, in her Decay.

Horace Walpole acknowledged his fellow gardener's horticultural work of art, commenting that Pope had 'rhymed and harmonised' his 'little bit of ground'.

If the contributions of these men to the villas and grounds of Chiswick and Marble Hill are still accessible for public appreciation, their own individual projects are more obscure. Walpole's Gothic castle now houses a teacher-training college, and the remains of Pope's fabled grotto lie in the grounds of a private school.

Down House

*Charles Darwin,
photograph by Julia Margaret Cameron,
1868.*

RIGHT **Darwin's study at
Down House.**

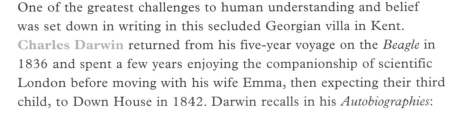

One of the greatest challenges to human understanding and belief
was set down in writing in this secluded Georgian villa in Kent.
Charles Darwin returned from his five-year voyage on the *Beagle* in
1836 and spent a few years enjoying the companionship of scientific
London before moving with his wife Emma, then expecting their third
child, to Down House in 1842. Darwin recalls in his *Autobiographies*:

> After several fruitless searches in Surrey and elsewhere, we found
> this house and purchased it. I was pleased with the diversified
> appearance of the vegetation proper to the chalk district, and so
> unlike what I had been accustomed to in the Midland counties;
> and still more pleased with the extreme quietness and rusticity of
> the place.

Darwin had returned from his long voyage with evidence that living things are not fixed and unchanging, but evolve over time. He was by no means the first to propose the notion of evolution: his grandfather Erasmus Darwin had even expounded the idea. But it was Charles Darwin who formulated in *On the Origin of Species* (1859) the mechanism by which evolution could happen:

ABOVE **Down House, built in the late 18th century, remains much as it was when Darwin lived here.**

> … if useful variations occur, individuals thus characterised will have the best chance of being preserved in the struggle for life; and from the strong principle of inheritance, these will tend to produce offspring similarly characterised. This principle of preservation, or the survival of the fittest, I have called Natural Selection. It leads to the improvement of each creature in relation to its conditions of life; and consequently, in most cases, to what must be regarded as an advance in organisation.

Darwin was not eager to publish findings so at odds with public opinion in general and his wife's ardent Christian beliefs in particular, but a letter he received in 1858 from naturalist Alfred Russel Wallace prompted him to action. Wallace had independently discovered the principle of natural selection unaware of Darwin's work, and the idea entered the public domain with a joint paper read to the Linnean Society later that year. Wallace was always happy for Darwin to take the credit for the discovery, and he later parted company with their theory, arguing that the human mind had spiritual rather than evolutionary origins.

Like Darwin, Samuel Butler had given up earlier plans to become a clergyman in favour of other pursuits. He exhibited paintings at the Royal Academy and tried his hand at musical composition, but he is best known for his satirical novel *Erewhon* (1870), and the autobiographical novel *The Way of All Flesh* (published posthumously in 1902). Butler was initially excited by Darwin's ideas; they corresponded for a while, with Butler becoming a frequent visitor to Down House. But like Wallace, Butler went on to develop different views, expounding these publicly in what became a one-sided argument. His book *Life and Habit*, which had started out as a supplement to Darwin's *Origin*, launched on its publication in 1878 an attack on Darwin's central idea. But Butler was an original thinker in other ways, too, coming to the conclusion that Homer's *Iliad* and *Odyssey* had in fact been written by a woman.

Butler's visits to Down eventually came to an end as a result of the two men's ideological disagreement. By contrast, Darwin's granddaughter, the artist Gwen Raverat, remembers her own visits there with happiness and affection in her autobiographical *Period Piece* (1952). Gwen, who became well known as a wood-engraver, was the daughter of the Darwins' second son, George. Though she was born three years after Charles's death, her memoir conjures a strong sense of the great man's presence around the house:

> Of all places at Down, the Sandwalk seemed most to belong to my grandfather. It was a path running round a little wood which he had planted himself; and it always seemed to be a very long way from the house. You went right to the furthest end of the kitchen garden, and then through a wooden door in the high hedge, which quite cut you off from human society. Here a fenced path ran along between two great lonely meadows, till you came to the wood … it was very lonely there.

Rochester Castle and
Historic Dockyard, Chatham

In the diary he kept for nine years from the age of 27, Samuel Pepys gives a detailed and personal account of his work as clerk of the acts to the Navy Board, a central role in what was then a very important government department. In October 1665, on one of many visits to the Chatham dockyards, he also visited Rochester Castle:

> Thence to Rochester; walked to the Crowne, and while dinner was getting ready, I did there walk to visit the old castle ruins, which hath been a noble place; and there going up, I did upon the stairs overtake three pretty maids or women and took them up with me, and I did besarlas muchas vezes et tocar leur mains and necks, to my great pleasure: but, Lord, to see what a dreadful thing it is to look down praecipices, for it did fright me mightily and hinder me of much pleasure which I would have made to myself in the company of these three if it had not been for that. The place hath been very noble, and great and strong in former ages.

Pepys's diary (1660–9) was a secret endeavour, written in shorthand, so it is curious that he bothered to use foreign words as an additional smokescreen when describing his various sexual adventures. Confident of its privacy, Pepys is absorbingly honest about every aspect of his character, even recording his acceptance of bribes and his acts of personal cowardice.

As well as being a uniquely frank sketch of an individual personality, Pepys's diary bears witness to some of the key historical events of the time: the Plague and the Great Fire, and then, in June 1667, the destruction of the English fleet in the Medway. Pepys records the impression the news made on all who heard it:

> Ill news is come to Court of the Dutch breaking the chaine at Chatham, which struck me to the heart, and to Whitehall to hear the truth of it; and there, going up the park stairs, I did hear some lackeys speaking of sad news come to Court, saying that hardly anybody in the court but doth look as if they cried.

Pepys discontinued his diary when difficulty with close work made him fear that he was going blind. Fortunately his fear was groundless,

though it meant that the remaining thirty-four years of his life were to pass tantalisingly unrecorded.

Like many Englishmen of his time, the Pepys who had cheered as a schoolboy when the king's head was cut off managed not merely to reconcile himself to the restoration of Charles II but to thrive under it. Not so the staunch Parliamentarian Celia Fiennes, the tone of whose *Journal* so often emphasises that this was a lady not for turning. Celia passed through Rochester some thirty years after Pepys on her 1697 journey, noting in her *Journal* a description of the Chatham dockyards as well as Rochester Castle:

> The town is large includeing the suburbs and all, for there is a
> large place before you pass the river, which washes quite round
> that side of the town to the Dock yards, that a mile from it, where
> are two large yards for building ships; I saw severall large shipps
> building others refitting; there was in one place a sort of arches
> like a bridge of brick-work, they told me the use of it was to let in
> the water there and so they put their masts in to season; besides

ABOVE Built on Rochester's Roman city walls, on the site of an earlier timber fortress, the castle was a vital stronghold, and was rebuilt by both Henry III and Edward I. It is seen here from the River Medway.

this dock here are severall streetes of houses on this hill which is pretty high and is just against Rochester, and on the hill you have the best prospect of the town and see the severall good Churches in it, and the Castle which is a pretty little thing, just by the Medway, which runs along by it and so at foote of this hill in a round, and so onward to the sea ...

William Cobbett arrived in Chatham in 1784 intending to go to sea, but in the event he enlisted as a soldier and served for the next seven years. After obtaining his discharge, Cobbett began writing as an anti-radical, but here was someone whose views changed enormously as a result of personal observation and experience, and his *Rural Rides* take a vigorous swipe at many of the injustices of the day.

Rochester and Chatham both make appearances in the novels of **Charles Dickens**. Dickens was the son of a clerk in the navy pay office, and his happiest childhood years, from 1817 to 1821, were spent in Chatham, before his father was imprisoned for debt and he, at the age of 12, had to take a job in a blacking warehouse. In *The Pickwick Papers*, which achieved great success for the 25-year-old author, Dickens describes the visit of Mr Pickwick and friends to Chatham and Rochester. Pickwick pontificates about the features of the Medway towns:

'The streets present a lively and animated appearance, occasioned chiefly by the conviviality of the military. It is truly delightful to a philanthropic mind to see these gallant men staggering along under the influence of an overflow both of animal and ardent spirits; more especially when we remember that the following them about, and jesting with them, affords a cheap and innocent amusement for the boy population. Nothing,' adds Mr. Pickwick, 'can exceed their good-humour. It was but the day before my arrival that one of them had been most grossly insulted in the house of a publican. The barmaid had positively refused to draw him any more liquor; in return for which he had (merely in playfulness) drawn his bayonet, and wounded the girl in the shoulder. And yet this fine fellow was the very first to go down to the house next morning and express his readiness to overlook the matter, and forget what had occurred!

LEFT The doorway
between the great hall
and the chamber.

'The consumption of tobacco in these towns,' continues Mr.
Pickwick, 'must be very great, and the smell which pervades
the streets must be exceedingly delicious to those who are
extremely fond of smoking. A superficial traveller might
object to the dirt, which is their leading characteristic; but to
those who view it as an indication of traffic and commercial
prosperity, it is truly gratifying.'

When Pickwick and Snodgrass catch sight, later in the book, of
Rochester Castle, their companion Jingle exclaims, 'Glorious pile –
frowning walls – tottering arches – dark nooks – crumbling staircases',
and Dickens draws on other areas of the town in many of his later
novels, notably *Great Expectations*, where Miss Havisham's home, Satis
House, is based on Restoration House in Maidstone Road.

Dover Castle

Shakespeare's *King Lear* follows the fortunes of two old men who misjudge their children and come to grief. Lear tries to discover which of his daughters loves him the most, rejecting the honest but less silver-tongued Cordelia in favour of her sisters, Goneril and Regan. Meanwhile the Duke of Gloucester believes the word of his bastard son, Edmund, that the other, legitimate, son, Edgar, is plotting to kill him. Innocent Edgar flees, disguising himself as the madman, Poor Tom. Gloucester, betrayed by Edmund, has had his eyes put out, and asks Poor Tom to lead him to a cliff near Dover, where he intends to leap to his death.

Not realising that Poor Tom is Edgar, Gloucester is led to the edge of the cliff by his faithful son:

> Come on, sir; here's the place. Stand still. How fearful
> And dizzy 'tis to cast one's eyes so low!
> The crows and choughs that wing the midway air
> Show scarce so gross as beetles. Halfway down
> Hangs one that gathers samphire: dreadful trade;
> Methinks he seems no bigger than his head.
> The fishermen that walk upon the beach
> Appear like mice ...

Edgar talks the old man out of this course of action and looks after him until his death. Lear, though, is too late to save Cordelia from Edmund's scheming, and the play ends with the king and all his daughters dead.

In 1802, **William Wordsworth** travelled to Calais with his sister Dorothy to visit his illegitimate daughter Caroline and her French mother, Annette. Dorothy remembers in her journal:

> ... seeing far off in the west the coast of England like a cloud crested with Dover Castle which was but like the summit of the cloud – the evening star and the glory of the sky.

Wordsworth had visited revolutionary France twice, falling in love with Annette, the daughter of a surgeon, in 1791. Their forced separation after his return to England was made more difficult by the declaration of war between their two countries in 1793. Although he never wrote directly about this passionate and turbulent time in his life, the famous couplet from the Prelude about revolutionary Paris probably owes as much to being in love as to political fervour:

Bliss was it in that dawn to be alive,
But to be young was very heaven!

Wordsworth's 1802 sonnet, written during this visit to Calais – a visit made possible by the Peace of Amiens – reflects as so often the observations recorded by Dorothy:

Fair Star of evening, Splendour of the west,
Star of my Country! – on the horizon's brink
Thou hangest, stooping, as might seem, to sink
On England's bosom …

BELOW There has been a castle at Dover since William I, in 1066, strengthened the defences of an Anglo-Saxon fortress. The castle that survives today, with its monumental keep, was built in the 1180s by Henry II.

When the self-educated William Cobbett visited Dover, he identified the cliff described in Shakespeare's play, thinking it 'fearfully steep' and 'very nearly perpendicular'.

His *Rural Rides* entry for 3 September 1823 contains this verbal sketch of the town and its castle:

> The town of Dover is like other sea-port towns; but really much more clean, and with less blackguard people in it than I ever observed in any sea-port before. It is a most picturesque place, to be sure. On one side of it rises, upon the top of a very steep hill, the Old Castle, with all its fortifications. On the other side of it there is another chalk hill, the side of which rises up from sixty to a hundred feet higher than the tops of the houses, which stand pretty close to the foot of the hill.

If Cobbett was awed by the landscape, he was not impressed by the Royal Military Canal. This had been built in 1809 to help protect the town, which was considered vulnerable to attack even though the castle had been strengthened. 'Those armies that had so often crossed the Rhine and the Danube were to be kept back by a canal', is his sharp dismissal of the English defences.

Part of Matthew Arnold's poem *Dover Beach* (1867) was written while he was on honeymoon in the town, en route to the Continent. Arnold's father, Dr Thomas Arnold, was the headmaster of Rugby School immortalised in Thomas Hughes's *Tom Brown's Schooldays*, and in 1851, the year of his marriage, Matthew himself embarked on a career as an inspector of schools that was to last thirty-five years. This poem was one of the last he was to write, before turning his attention to literary criticism, and to religious works.

> The sea is calm to-night,
> The tide is full, the moon lies fair
> Upon the straits; - on the French coast the light
> Gleams and is gone; the cliffs of England stand,
> Glimmering and vast, out in the tranquil bay.

Where Dover inspires in Arnold an impassioned contemplation of the loss of Christian faith in England, W H Auden's poem *Dover* takes a political and historical view, offering a down-to-earth description of the town, whose sea-front he calls 'almost elegant':

A Norman castle, dominant, flood-lit at night,
Trains which fume in a station built on the sea,
Testify to the interests of its regular life ...

Auden's picture of Dover presents a microcosm of England, a country 'of minor importance', with 'half its history done'. But Auden's poetry, too, was to become much more Christian in tone, and he even altered or disowned some of his earlier political works. Although he spent the war years in America, Auden did return to England, and was elected professor of poetry at Oxford in 1956.

Pevensey Castle and Battle Abbey

RIGHT **Pevensey Castle is one of Britain's oldest strongholds, with fortifications surviving from both the Roman and the medieval periods.**

Stories inspired by his travels in India and Africa are those for which **Rudyard Kipling** is most famous: *The Jungle Book* (1894) and *Just So Stories* (1897–1902). But Kipling finally settled at Bateman's, an old house near Burwash, in 1902, and some of the nearby Sussex sites feature in his *Puck of Pook's Hill*, published in 1906.

This is a story in which various episodes of the past are magically brought to life for Dan and Una, after they perform *A Midsummer Night's Dream* three times inside a fairy ring, and are surprised by Puck appearing from the bushes. He entertains them by conjuring up various characters to tell their stories, including a Roman centurion at Hadrian's Wall and a Norman knight. The knight, Sir Richard, tells of how, in the days after the death of William the Conqueror, 'we bore gold to Pevensey on horseback – three loads of it – and then up to the north chamber, above the Great Hall of Pevensey Castle'. The castle is brought to life in Sir Richard's tale: 'Pevensey walls are strong. No man ... knows what is between them', and the children hear that 'the Great Hall is always bitter cold'.

One character in the knight's colourful tale is 'Gilbert, a clerk from Battle Abbey, who kept the accounts of the Manor of Pevensey'. An anonymous version of the founding of the abbey, *The Chronicle of Battle Abbey*, was written in Latin around 1180. It begins with William's landing 'near the town called Pevensey', and proceeding 'with his men to a near-by port called Hastings' where he 'found a suitable place, and with foresight he quickly built a wooden fort'. An even earlier work, attributed to Bishop Guy of Amiens, is believed to be the first Latin poem written for the Anglo-Norman court. *Carmen Hastingae Proelio*, or *Song of the Battle of Hastings*, was probably written in 1067, and it vividly describes the beginning of the Norman invasion:

> One of the English, lying hidden close to a sea-rock, perceived how the countless ranks spread far and wide and saw the fields glittering, full of glancing arms. He saw the people, their homes ravaged by flames for their perfidy, perish by the raging sword, and what tears the children shed for their fathers' slaughter. He ran to mount a horse and sped to tell the king.

BELOW The stone vaulting of the monks' common room at Battle Abbey. The abbey was built by William I in 1070, to atone for the bloodshed of the Norman Conquest.

According to the *Carmen*, in the aftermath of the battle 'the corpses of the English, strewn on the ground, he left to be devoured by worms and wolves'. The victorious William then remained at Hastings for a fortnight before making his way towards Dover.

The writer of *Rural Rides*, William Cobbett, visited Battle in January 1822, but his account of it reads more like the experience of a modern-day businessman than that of a crusading rural investigator, and it was the local hostelry rather than the abbey that absorbed his attention:

> Got home from Battle. I had no time to see the town, having entered the Inn on Wednesday in the dusk of the evening, having been engaged all day yesterday in the Inn, and having come out of it, only to get into the coach this morning.

Bayham Old Abbey

It may not be unusual for a politician to write a best-selling novel, but we do not generally associate literary innovation with the Palace of Westminster. Yet the writer who invented the Gothic novel was an MP, and son to Britain's first Prime Minister. Horace Walpole began his parliamentary career when he returned from his grand tour of Europe in 1741, and after his father's death four years later he was able to purchase a former coachman's cottage near Twickenham in Middlesex: Strawberry Hill. For over twenty years the rebuilding of this house in the Gothic style was Walpole's chief preoccupation, and the house, which stood in an estate of forty-six acres, eventually extended to twenty-two rooms.

It is not surprising that Walpole encountered Gothic imagery in his sleep, so steeped was he in this style of art and architecture:

> I waked one morning at the beginning of last June from a dream, of which all I could recover was, that I had thought myself in an ancient castle (a very natural dream for a head filled like mine with Gothic story) and that on the uppermost bannister of a great staircase I saw a gigantic hand in armour. In the evening I sat down and began to write, without knowing in the least what I intended to say or relate. The work grew on my hands, and I grew fond of it - add that I was very glad to think of anything rather than politics - in short I was so engrossed in my tale, which I completed in less than two months, that one evening I wrote from the time I had drunk my tea, about six o'clock, till half an hour after one in the morning, when my hand and fingers were so weary, that I could not hold the pen to finish the sentence …

This was to be the first Gothic novel, a genre Walpole invented and named. Such was his absorption in the book that he took it with him when visiting Bayham Abbey, where much of *The Castle of Otranto* (1765) was written. The novel purports to be the translation of a recovered Italian document, and is so extraordinary in its effects that it reads almost as a parody of the genre it was bringing into being:

> 'Ah, me, I am slain!' cried Matilda, sinking. 'Good heaven, receive my soul!'

'Savage, inhuman monster, what hast thou done!' cried Theodore, rushing on him, and wrenching his dagger from him.

'Stop, stop thy impious hand!' cried Matilda; 'it is my father!'

Manfred, waking as from a trance, beat his breast, twisted his hands in his locks, and endeavoured to recover his dagger from Theodore to despatch himself. Theodore, scarce less distracted, and only mastering the transports of his grief to assist Matilda, had now by his cries drawn some of the monks to his aid. While part of them endeavoured, in concert with the afflicted Theodore, to stop the blood of the dying Princess, the rest prevented Manfred from laying violent hands on himself.

LEFT Bayham Old Abbey: the ruins of a monastery founded for the order of the 'White Canons' in about 1208.

The killing of Matilda by her father Manfred, the tyrant of Otranto, is an episode towards the end of a long and convoluted plot. The walls of the castle crumble and a huge statue of the usurped prince rises to heaven, before Theodore, Otranto's rightful heir, is restored to power.

Afraid that he would be ridiculed for the novel, Walpole had it published under a pseudonym, but its immediate and huge success meant that he soon felt able to step forward as its author. There were no further novels, but Walpole wrote books about history and gardening as well as conducting a prodigious correspondence with around 200 friends and acquaintances. Walpole's Gothic castle was sold off after his death, and the building now houses a college; but his Gothic novel has inspired a host of imitations and parodies, from Mary Shelley's *Frankenstein* to Jane Austen's *Northanger Abbey*.

Royal Garrison Church

The chancel of a 13th-century church in Portsmouth survived the 1941 firebomb raid that destroyed much of the building. This church, known as the Royal Garrison Church, is the model for that in which the family of Fanny Price worshipped in Jane Austen's *Mansfield Park* (1814).

Fanny Price, often said to be Jane Austen's least attractive heroine, is a sickly and timid creature, rescued from her lower-middle-class family by an aunt who has made a more advantageous marriage, Lady Bertram. But the only member of the family to show Fanny any consideration is cousin Edmund, and they become close friends. Then Henry and Mary Crawford, smart young people from London, arrive as guests, compromising the order of the house by drawing the young Bertrams into amateur theatricals. Edmund becomes attracted to Mary, and Henry flirts with and proposes to Fanny. However, to the Bertrams' astonishment Fanny refuses what they consider to be an excellent offer, and is sent back to her chaotic family home in Portsmouth to take stock of her situation. It is here that Henry Crawford visits her:

Jane Austen,
portrait by Cassandra Austen,
circa 1810.

> The Prices were just setting off for church the next day when Mr Crawford appeared again. He came – not to stop – but to join them; he was asked to go with them to the Garrison chapel, which is exactly what he had intended, and they all walked thither together ...
>
> In chapel they were obliged to divide, but Mr Crawford took care not to be divided from the female branch; and after chapel he still continued with them, and made one in the family party on the ramparts.

Despite Henry's attentions Fanny remains determined, and when Edmund finally sees Mary in her true colours, the cousins are united.

Jane Austen was herself born and raised in Hampshire, moving with her family to Bath in 1801. Her father, a Tory parson, encouraged Jane's reading and writing, but her six great novels all appeared after his death. This event in 1806 occasioned the family's move back to Hampshire, and they finally settled in the village of Chawton. It was here, in the busy parlour, that *Mansfield Park*, *Emma* and *Persuasion* were written.

LEFT The east window in the chancel.

ABOVE The Royal Garrison Church in Portsmouth was constructed in about 1212 as a hostel for pilgrims, becoming a garrison church in the 1560s. The church was badly damaged by a firebomb in 1941, but the chancel survived.

Titchfield Abbey

RIGHT Founded for the order of the 'White Canons' in 1232, Titchfield Abbey and its estate passed in 1537, following the Dissolution of the Monasteries, to Thomas Wriothesley, Earl of Southampton. He converted it into a grand residence, characterised by this massive Tudor gatehouse.

> Shall I compare thee to a summer's day?
> Thou art more lovely and more temperate.

The person to whom William Shakespeare addressed his most famous sonnet was never specifically identified by the poet, but most scholars now believe it to have been Henry Wriothesley, third Earl of Southampton, whose ancestral home was Titchfield Abbey.

From his portraits it is evident that Wriothesley was a beautiful young man, with auburn hair and blue eyes, and we know that in his late teens, the age at which it was considered appropriate to marry, Wriothesley was disinclined to do so. He even chose to pay a hefty £5,000 fine rather than go ahead with a marriage to Elizabeth de Vere, granddaughter of his guardian, Lord Burghley.

We also know that Wriothesley was Shakespeare's patron: the two long poems, *Venus and Adonis* and *The Rape of Lucrece* are dedicated to him with exceptional warmth, but the sonnets were ambiguously dedicated 'to the onlie begetter of these insuing sonnets Mr W H ...', prompting the suggestion that the initials were reversed to conceal the begetter's identity.

The sonnet was enjoying great popularity at court in the 1590s, and Shakespeare seems to have begun composing in the form early in the decade, with some of the poems circulating in manuscript amongst his friends. These are the only works in which the poet uses the first person singular, which has led to the supposition that a great deal of their emotional content is autobiographical.

It would not have been unusual for a poet to address his patron as muse, but the first 17 of the 126 poems addressed to a young man attempt to persuade him to marry and have children:

> Look in thy glass and tell the face thou viewest
> Now is the time that face should form another,
> Whose fresh repair if now thou not renewest
> Thou dost beguile the world, unbless some mother …

What is unusual is the boldness with which the speaker addresses his subject on topics of such an intimate nature, and also the passion and consistency with which he professes not just his friendship and gratitude, but his love:

> O know, sweet love, I always write of you,
> And you and love are still my argument …

Henry Wriothesley, Thomas's grandson and the third Earl of Southampton; painting after Daniel Mytens, circa 1618.

Eventually, at the relatively late age of 25, Henry Wriothesley accepted his duty to the family line. But his hasty marriage to Elizabeth Vernon, cousin of the Earl of Essex and lady-in-waiting to the Queen, resulted in the angry monarch offering post-nuptial accommodation in Fleet prison.

With Wriothesley as his patron, it is likely that Shakespeare was a regular visitor to Titchfield Abbey. The site had been rebuilt as a mansion by Henry's grandfather in 1542, and it is thought that a number of plays were premiered there, including *Romeo and Juliet*, *Twelfth Night* and *A Midsummer Night's Dream*.

With the accession of James I in 1603, both men thrived. Shakespeare's sonnets were published in 1609, and by the end of his life he had written some thirty-seven plays. Henry Wriothesley fathered a son and a daughter, became involved with the British East India Company, and achieved the position of privy councillor. In 1624 he volunteered with his son to lead an expedition to fight for the Netherlands against Spain, but during the campaign both he and his son died of fever. Henry Wriothesley is buried at Titchfield, and immortalised by England's greatest poet:

> So long as men can breathe or eyes can see,
> So long lives this, and this gives life to thee.

Netley Abbey

In 1533, librarian and poet John Leland began a ten-year tour through England to find material for a projected great work on the history and antiquities of the nation. However, Leland's task was never completed: he became insane in 1550, leaving an enormous quantity of notes, which were finally published as *Leland's Itinerary* in 1710. Among them, Leland left a brief note of Netley – then known as Letelege – Abbey:

> Scant a mile from the mouth of Hamelrise Creeke lyithe Letelege on the shore upward in the mayne haven.
> Here a late was a great abbay in building of White Monkes.

The ruins of this 13th-century abbey, and the legends that surround it, probably inspired not only the first true Gothic novel, but also the genre's best-known spoof. In a letter of 1755, Horace Walpole eulogises about the site:

> The ruins are vast, and retain fragments of beautiful fretted roofs pendent in the air, with all variety of Gothic patterns of windows wrapped round and round with ivy – many trees are sprouted up among the walls, and only want to be increased with cypresses!
> … In short, they are not the ruins of Netley, but of paradise …

Walpole visited Netley Abbey on several occasions, no doubt collecting ideas for his own 'little Gothic castle' that he had been building at Strawberry Hill in Twickenham, his home since 1747. On a visit in 1764 he was accompanied by his friend, the poet Thomas Gray, best known for his *Elegy in a Country Churchyard*. Gray is impressed not only by the building, but by the stories that surround it:

> The ferryman who rowed me, a lusty young Fellow, told me, that he would not for all the world pass a night at the Abbey, (there were such things seen near it,) tho' there was a power of money hid there.

The year after this visit Walpole's *Castle of Otranto* was published, a tale teeming with supernatural entities and torrid emotions. Walpole confessed, 'I gave free rein to my imagination; visions and passions

LEFT The first Cistercian monks entered the abbey at Netley in 1239. The grandeur of the church may be the consequence of the patronage of Henry III, but this did not protect the abbey during the Dissolution, when it was converted into a large Tudor house. By 1700 the building had fallen out of use, and the ruins became the inspiration for scores of writers.

RIGHT View looking down the nave of the church from the east.

chocked me', but he insisted on the novel appearing under a pseudonym, for fear of ridicule. He need not have worried; the book was an immediate success and spawned a host of imitators as well as parodists.

Gray's great poem was inspired not by Netley but by the churchyard at Stoke Poges. But as the influence of the Romantic movement arrived from Continental Europe, other poets were drawn to immortalise the abbey's atmospheric ruins. William Bowles, according to Byron 'the maudlin prince of sonneteers', composed one of his sonnets (1789) to the site:

> Fallen pile! I ask not what has been thy fate:
> But when the winds, wafted from the main,
> Through each lone arch, like spirits that complain,
> Come hollow to my ear, I meditate
> On this world's passing pageant, and the lot
> Of those who once might proudly in their prime,
> Stood smiling at decay, till bowed by time
> Or injury, their early boast forgot,
> They might have fallen like thee! Pale and forlorn
> Their brow, besprent with thin hairs, white as snow
> They lift, still unsubdued, as they would scorn
> This short-lived scene of vanity and woe
> Whilst on their sad looks smilingly they bear
> The trace of creeping age and the pale hue of care.

A year later, in 1790, the abbey was honoured with an ode by the poet and literary figure William Sotheby, *Netley Abbey: Midnight*:

> Within the sheltered centre of the aisle,
> Beneath the ash whose growth romantic spreads
> Its foliage trembling o'er the funeral pile,
> And all around a deeper darkness sheds;
> While through yon arch, where the thick ivy twines,
> Bright on the silvered tower the moon-beam shines,
> And the grey cloister's roofless length illumes,
> Upon the mossy stone I lie reclined,
> And to a visionary world resigned
> Call the pale spectres forth from the forgotten tombs …

But the excesses of Gothic sensibility were soon to come under the sharp scrutiny of Jane Austen. In a letter, the novelist's niece Fanny Knight writes about a visit made by the family to the abbey:

> We all except Grandmama, took a boat and went to Netley
> Abbey the ruins of which look beautiful. We ate some biscuits
> we had taken, and returned home quite delighted.

Jane may well have read Richard Warner's *Netley Abbey, a Gothic Story in two volumes*, a medieval tale published in 1795, because three years later she began the novel that was to become a Gothic parody, and her first completed work (though it was not published until 1817, following her death). It is possible that it was with her own family's visit in mind that Jane subsequently wrote of Catherine Morland in *Northanger Abbey*:

> As they drew near the end of their journey, her impatience
> for the sight of the abbey … returned in full force, and every
> bend on the road was expected with solemn awe to afford a
> glimpse of its massy walls of grey stone, rising amidst a grove
> of great oaks, with the last beams of the sunset playing in
> beautiful splendour in its high gothic wonders.

Another less effusive visitor to the abbey was political radical William Cobbett. When he was writing in 1830, it was the etymology of the name rather than the abbey's ivy-clad arches that drew his attention, in a comment that recalls Leland's note on the site:

Netley Abbey ought, it seems, to be called Letley Abbey, the
Latin name being Laetus Locus or Pleasant Place. Letley was
made up of an abbreviation of the Latin Laetus and of the
Saxon word ley, which meant place, field, or piece of land.

With his usual nonconformist contempt, Cobbett also referred to the
dissolution of the abbey by Henry VIII:

The possessions of these monks were by the wife killing founder
of the Church of England, given away (although they belonged to
the public) to one of his court sycophants.

Though born in neighbouring Surrey, Cobbett was a Hampshire
resident for fifteen years from 1805. In the village of Botley he tried
various farming ventures, many of which proved to be financial disasters,
such as an attempt to rear merino sheep. His bold endeavour was
thwarted by the damp conditions prevalent in the Hampshire basin.

It was the discovery of some female human remains at the abbey that
prompted one of the verse tales in Reverend Richard Barham's
Ingoldsby Legends. First published in 1837 in *Bentley's Miscellany*, edited
by his friend Charles Dickens, these mostly comic narrative verses
were an enormous popular success for over a century. Barham's story
here is reminiscent of canto 6 of Scott's *Marmion*, in which Constance
de Beverley is walled up alive in Lindisfarne:

And there was an ugly hole in the wall
For an oven too big for a cellar too small.
And I said 'Here's a nun has been playing some tricks'
That horrible hole! It seems to say
I'm a grave that gapes for a living prey!

Ah me, ah me tis sad to think
That maiden's eye which was made to blink
Should here be compelled to grow blear and blink
Or be closed for aye. In this kind of way
Shut out for ever from wholesome day.
Walled up in a hole with never a chink
No light – no air – no victuals – no drink.

That wandering glance and furtive kiss
Exceedingly naughty and wrong I wis
Should yet be considered so much amiss
As to call for a sentence severe as this
And I said to myself as I heard with a sigh
The poor lone victim's stifled cry
Well I can't understand how any man's hand
Could wall up that hole in a Christian land …

Barham, despite the liveliness of his versifying, writes with a seriousness that precludes any Gothic atmospherics; and the concluding couplet is a powerful statement from the man who was once a minor canon at St Paul's.

LEFT The south doorway to the church.

Carisbrooke Castle

It is surely a very ungrateful guest who would try to escape from his comfortable lodging in this magnificent Norman castle, particularly when a bowling green has been made expressly for his enjoyment. But that is precisely what Charles I tried – and failed – to do. Celia Fiennes, intrepid traveller and staunch Cromwellian, visited the castle sometime in the late 1680s, forty years after these events, but the royal incarceration is uppermost in her mind as she commits her description of the place, in inimitable style, to her *Journal*. Celia's point of reference is the town of Newport, on the Isle of Wight:

> A mile off it is Carsbrooke Castle into which King Charles the first retired when he was worsted by the Parliaments forces; there are some good roomes still that remaine but the most part are destroyed and only ruined walls to be seen, there is a deep well of 40 fathom, they draw up the bucket by a great Wheele in which they put a horse or ass, a stone thrown down sounds a long tyme ere you hear it splash into the water.

What seem 'only ruined walls' to this late-17th-century traveller were an inspiration to a poet of the early 19th century. John Keats spent a brief holiday on the island in April 1817, staying at Mrs Cook's in what is now Castle Road, with a view of the castle from his window. In an enthusiastic letter to his friend and fellow poet John Reynolds, he writes:

> I have not seen many specimens of Ruins - I dont think however I shall ever see one to surpass Carisbrooke Castle. The trench is o'ergrown with the smoothest turf, and the Walls with ivy - The Keep within side is one Bower of ivy - a Colony of Jackdaws have been there many years. I dare say I have seen many a descendant of some old cawer who peeped through the Bars at Charles the first, when he was there in Confinement.

Keats had met Reynolds at the London home of Leigh Hunt the previous year, and Reynolds was to become his advocate and supporter through years of public criticism and private difficulty. In the letter Keats explains how necessary poetry is to him:

> I find that I cannot exist without poetry ... I had become
> all in a Tremble from not having written any thing of late –

But this lean poetic phase came to an end while Keats was staying at Carisbrooke. Here he began his great long poem *Endymion*, and composed the Petrarchan sonnet *On the Sea*:

> It keeps eternal whisperings around
> Desolate shores, and with its mighty swell
> Gluts twice ten thousand caverns, till the spell
> Of Hecate leaves them their old shadowy sound.
> Often 'tis in such gentle temper found,
> That scarcely will the very smallest shell
> Be moved for days from whence it sometime fell,
> When last the winds of heaven were unbound.
> Oh ye! who have your eye-balls vexed and tired,
> Feast them upon the wideness of the Sea;
> Oh ye! whose ears are dinned with uproar rude,
> Or fed too much with cloying melody, -
> Sit ye near some old cavern's mouth, and brood
> Until ye start, as if the sea-nymphs choired!

Only four years later, in the advanced stages of consumption, Keats made the journey by sea to Italy in the hope of restoring his health, but he died in Rome at the age of 25.

According to one account of Charles I's sojourn at Carisbrooke Castle, the king rashly offered the governor a priceless diamond in exchange for his freedom. But the governor was none other than Colonel John Mohune – 'Blackbeard' – who double-crossed the king, and was then discovered himself. Before his arrest, however, he managed to conceal the diamond somewhere in the castle ...

The discovery of Blackbeard's diamond by the young John Trenchard and his taciturn friend Elzevir Block is set against a tale of smuggling on the Dorset coast in John Meade Falkner's *Moonfleet* (1898). Trenchard, the narrator, is an older, sadder man than the youth, his younger self, whose adventures he is relating, and there is trial and tragedy as the story unfolds.

Fifteen-year-old Trenchard's chance discovery of Blackbeard's locket and the parchment within finally leads him and Elzevir, a smuggler, to the Isle of Wight:

We were very hot and soaking wet when we stood at the gateway of Carisbrooke Castle. Here are two flanking towers and a stout gate-house reached by a stone bridge crossing the moat; and when I saw it I remembered that 'twas here Colonel Mohune had earned the wages of his unrighteousness, and thought how many times he must have passed these gates.

The clues on the parchment take them through the castle and into a 'square building of stone with a high roof like the large dove-cots that you may see in old stackyards': the well-house. Here, Trenchard is lowered into the well to retrieve the diamond, and they manage to escape to Holland to sell it. But they are tricked, captured and sentenced to hard labour on the galleys for life. Finally, shipwrecked while on a sea voyage to a penal settlement in Java, Trenchard is saved from drowning in Moonfleet bay by Elzevir, who loses his own life in the attempt.

Reminiscent in many respects of R L Stevenson's adventure novels, *Moonfleet* is an oddly neglected book. It was one of three written by Falkner, who worked for a Newcastle armaments manufacturer and wrote stories, and also poetry, in his spare time. When the draft of a fourth novel was stolen from a railway carriage, Falkner was not, by all accounts, unduly concerned. But *Moonfleet*, set in the Dorset of Falkner's boyhood, and with a central relationship to rival that between Jim Hawkins and Long John Silver, is an atmospheric and exciting read.

Waverley Abbey and Farnham Castle Keep

ABOVE **Waverley Abbey, the first Cistercian abbey to be established in England, was founded in 1128.**

The ruins of Waverley Abbey may have inspired and lent their name to **Sir Walter Scott**'s famous series of tales, yet none of the *Waverley Novels* is actually set there. The abbey will have been part of the daily life of the young **Jonathan Swift**, however, following his appointment to the post of secretary to Sir William Temple at nearby Moor Park in 1689. It was here that, at the age of 22, Swift met a sickly little 8-year-old girl who was to become his dearest friend, the love of his life, and possibly his wife.

Esther Johnson, whom Swift nicknamed Stella, was the daughter of a companion to Temple's sister, and Swift became her playmate and teacher. Impatient for preferment, Swift returned to his native Ireland in 1694 to be ordained, but returned to Moor Park two years later, to find the 15-year-old Esther grown 'beautiful, graceful and agreeable'.

After Temple's death, Swift persuaded her to live in his parish at Trim, near Dublin, which she did for the rest of her life. Swift's *Journal to Stella* is a collection of his intimate letters to her while he was in London from 1710 to 1713, and rumours abounded that the two had secretly married in 1716.

A teasing intimacy exists in the birthday poems Swift sent to Esther annually on 13 March. In 1719 he writes:

> Stella this day is thirty-four,
> (We shan't dispute a year or more:)
> However, Stella, be not troubled,
> Although thy size and years are doubled,
> Since first I saw thee at sixteen,
> The brightest virgin on the green ...

And the 1721 poem refers to her 'angel's face, a little cracked'. Swift could not bring himself to attend Esther's deathbed in 1728, but he is buried beside her in St Patrick's Cathedral, Dublin.

Waverley was also one of the childhood haunts of William Cobbett. He recalls in *Advice to Young Men and (Incidentally) to Young Women, in the Middle and Higher Ranks of Life* (1828) a day spent in the fields near Waverley Abbey – a moment he describes with a Wordsworthian intensity:

> When I was a very little boy, I was, in the barley-sowing season,
> going along by the side of a field, near Waverley Abbey; the
> primroses and bluebells bespangling the banks on both sides of
> me; a thousand linnets singing in the spreading oak over my
> head; while the jingling of the traces and the whistling of the
> ploughboy saluted my ear from over the hedge ... I was not more
> than eight years old; but this particular scene has presented itself
> to my mind many times every year from that day to this.'

ABOVE **This slender column in the abbey cellars still supports the vaulting after hundreds of years.**

Cobbett visited the abbey during his journeys on horseback through the south of England, which he wrote up in essay form as *Rural Rides* (published in 1830). The aim of these journeys was to observe the conditions of the rural poor, but when he is in the grounds of Waverley with his youngest son, Richard, further memories of boyhood flood back:

> I showed him a tree, close by the ruins of the Abbey, from a limb
> of which I once fell into the river, in an attempt to take the nest
> of a crow, which had artfully placed it upon a branch so far from
> the trunk, as not to be able to bear the weight of a boy eight years
> old ... I found the ruins not very greatly diminished; but, it is
> strange how small the mansion, and ground, and everything but
> the trees, appeared to me.

He does, however, notice some changes: 'the old monks' garden walls are totally gone, and the spot is become a sort of lawn.' Cobbett's characteristic humour and passionate interest in the land are evident in these passages, but they are strikingly different from the down-to-earth prose that is the hallmark of *Rural Rides*.

Cobbett is buried beside his father in St Andrew's churchyard in Farnham, not far from his birthplace in the Jolly Farmer Inn. After the Restoration, when Farnham Castle was in a more hospitable state of repair than in Cobbett's time, it had been home to one of England's early biographers, Izaak Walton.

Walton was an innkeeper's son who achieved status and prosperity through his own drapery business, though his personal life was full of tragedy: his first wife died in 1640, after each of their seven children had died in infancy. It was after the death of his second wife, a relative of Archbishop Cranmer, in 1662 that Walton became a resident of Farnham Castle as the permanent guest of the Bishop of Winchester.

Although he was widely read, Walton's career as a biographer was fortuitous. He had lived in the parish where John Donne was vicar and the men had been friends, so when Donne's biographer died leaving his

LEFT The outer walls at Farnham Castle Keep. This motte-and-bailey castle has been continuously occupied since the 12th century.

work unfinished, Walton completed it. He went on to write several other biographies, notably of another poet-priest who also happened to be his fishing companion – George Herbert.

Yet it was to be fishing and not biography that made Izaak Walton's literary reputation. In 1653 he published *The Compleat Angler*, his classic guidebook to the sport, a mixture of practical information, songs and quotations. It follows three friends, a huntsman, a fowler and a fisherman, as they travel through the English countryside, discussing the relative merits of their pursuits:

> We may say of angling, as Dr. Boteler said of strawberries,
> 'Doubtless God could have made a better berry, but doubtless
> God never did'; and so, if I might judge, God never did make a
> more calm, quiet, innocent recreation than angling.

The angler points out that 'Almighty God is said to have spoken to a fish, but never to a beast'. Such has been its popularity that, with over 300 impressions, *The Compleat Angler* is one of the most reprinted books in English literature.

Uffington Castle, White Horse, Dragon Hill and Wayland's Smithy

In the opening chapter of his novel *Tom Brown's Schooldays* (1857), Thomas Hughes devotes many pages to a detailed description of the Vale of White Horse, where both he and his eponymous hero grew up. His enthusiastic recalling of the 'fine range of chalk hills' and 'large rich pastures' sets the scene for a tour of some specific sites in the area he knew so well.

The first of these is the 'magnificent Roman camp' known as Uffington Castle. In fact, this is an Iron Age camp, though there is a Romano-British settlement nearby. Hughes gives an idiosyncratic account of the place, which was in his time 'as complete as it was twenty years after the strong old rogues left it'.

> Right up on the highest point, from which they say you can see eleven counties, they trenched round all the table-land, some twelve or fourteen acres, as was their custom, for they couldn't bear anybody to overlook them, and made their eyrie. The ground falls away rapidly on all sides. Was there ever such turf in the whole world? You sink up to your ankles at every step, and yet the spring of it is delicious. There is always a breeze in the 'camp' as it is called, and here it lies, just as the Romans left it ...

From the camp, Hughes descends towards the west, to a place that is 'sacred ground for Englishmen'. Hughes claims it to have been the site of the battle of Ashdown where, in 871, King Alfred 'broke the Danish power, and made England a Christian land'. Here, says Hughes,

> ... the pious King, that there might never be wanting a sign and a memorial to the country-side, carved out on the northern side of the chalk hill, under the camp, where it is most precipitous, the great Saxon white horse, which he who will may see from the railway, and which gives its name to the vale, over which it has looked these thousand years and more.

In fact, the precise site of the battle is not known, though Hughes, who was clearly drawn to myth-making, wrote an account of it in his fictional work *The Scouring of the White Horse* (1859). But in his *Ballad of the White Horse* (1911) G K Chesterton, best known for his Father Brown stories and celebration of a certain brand of Englishness, suggests that the monument is much older:

BELOW The dramatic figure of the White Horse, cut into the chalk hillside near the hillfort, is thought to date from the Iron Age. It measures 111 metres from the tip of its tail to its ear.

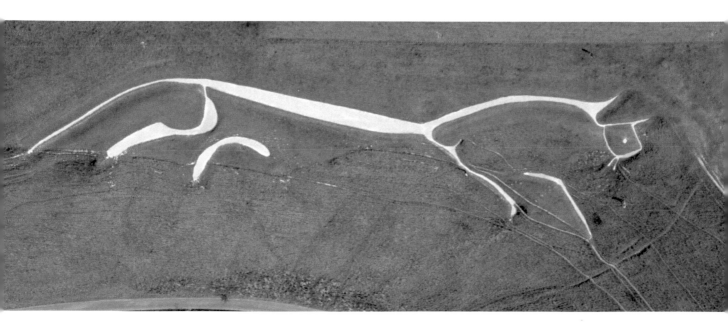

Before the gods that made the gods
Had seen their sunrise pass
The White Horse of the White Horse Vale
Was cut out of the grass.

Chesterton's verse is in line with recent studies that set the probable origin of the White Horse in the Bronze Age, making it around 3,000 years old.

The guided tour on which Hughes takes his reader in *Tom Brown's Schooldays* continues with a visit to Dragon Hill, 'a curious little round self-confident fellow':

> On this hill some deliverer of mankind – St George, the country folk used to tell me – killed a dragon. Whether it were St George, I cannot say; but surely a dragon was killed there, for you may see the marks yet where his blood ran down, and more by token the place where it ran down is the easiest way up the hill-side.

Hughes fishes yet another possibility from the myth-pool in *The Scouring of the White Horse*: that it might actually be Pendragon Hill, named after the chief of kings to the ancient Britons. A Liberal MP and co-founder of the Christian Socialist movement, Hughes extended his interest in the connection between heroic past and actual present to his personal view of Christianity. His adulation of Rugby headmaster Thomas Arnold and condemnation of the bullying Flashman in *Tom Brown's Schooldays* derived from a dislike of Christianity's image as a faith for the fearful, and he promulgated a combination of physical courage, sport, patriotism and Christian morality, the 'muscular Christianity' that had such an impact on subsequent public-school culture.

From Dragon Hill, Hughes guides his reader 'along the Ridgeway to the west for about a mile', to 'a little clump of young beech and firs'. In among them is Wayland Smith's cave:

ABOVE The mound of Dragon Hill nestles beneath the White Horse.

> ... an old cromlech, a huge flat stone raised on seven or eight others, and led up to by a path, with large single stones set up on each side.

This neolithic tomb was said to be the smithy of Wayland, the mythical farrier thought to haunt the Vale. But rather than engaging with the legend himself, Hughes refers his reader to Sir Walter Scott, and his novel *Kenilworth* (1821).

Smith, the character that Scott constructs, has many features of the legendary figure; 'a man in a farrier's leathern apron, but otherwise fantastically attired in a bear-skin dressed with the fur on, and a cap of the same'. His medicinal knowledge enables him to save the novel's heroine, Amy Robsart, from an attempt to poison her and it is Smith who escorts Amy on her ill-fated journey to Kenilworth. Amy's former love, the faithful Tressilian, is introduced to Smith at what he is informed is the door of the man's forge, but he can only see 'a bare moor, and that ring of stones, with a great one in the midst, like a Cornish barrow'. He is told:

You must tie your horse to that upright stone that has the ring in't, and then you must whistle three times, and lay me down your silver groat on that other flat stone, walk out of the circle, sit down on the west side of that little thicket of bushes, and take heed you look neither to right nor left for ten minutes, or so long as you shall hear the hammer clink, and whenever it ceases, say your prayers for the space you could tell a hundred, or count over a hundred, which will do as well, - and then come into the circle; you will find your money gone and your horse shod.

The practice Scott describes draws on the Celtic legend with which Rudyard Kipling was also familiar. According to Kipling's *Puck of Pook's Hill* (1906) Weland, or Wayland, was brought to England by Viking raiders, and Puck, another ancient mythical character, describes their first meeting:

> When he saw me he began a long chant in his own tongue, telling me how he was going to rule England, and how I should smell the smoke of his altars from Lincolnshire to the Isle of Wight.

Kipling's version of the story embellishes the Celtic and Norse myth, in which Weland is a smith to the gods: he cannot be released from his duty until he is wished well by a human. Puck and a novice from a nearby monastery persuade an unwilling farmer to do this and in gratitude Weland forges a sword with special powers, which he places in the hand of the sleeping novice.

ABOVE The Neolithic burial mound known as Wayland's Smithy dates from 4000 to 3000 BC. Upright sarsen stones flank the entrance to the chamber.

Index

Further reading

A list covering the most significant authors for English Heritage sites, and some works of particular interest.

Barker, Juliet 1994 *The Brontës*. London: Weidenfeld and Nicolson

Barker, Juliet (ed) 2002 *Wordsworth: A Life in Letters*. London: Viking

Bowman, Alan K 2003 *Life and Letters on the Roman Frontier – Vindolanda and its People*. London: British Museum

Butt, John (ed) 1960 *Letters of Alexander Pope*. London: Oxford University Press

Cobbett, William (edited by Ian Dyck) 2001 *Rural Rides*. London: Penguin

Daiches, David and Flower, John 1981 *Literary Landscapes of the British Isles: A Narrative Atlas*. Harmondsworth: Penguin

Drabble, Margaret (ed) 2003 (6th edition) *The Oxford Companion to English Literature*. Oxford: Oxford University Press

Fiennes, Celia (edited by Christopher Morris) 1995 *The Illustrated Journeys of Celia Fiennes 1685–1712*. Stroud: Alan Sutton

Geoffrey of Monmouth (translated from the Latin by Lewis Thorpe) 1976 *The History of the Kings of Britain*. London: Penguin

Gibson, James 1996 *Thomas Hardy: A Literary Life*. Basingstoke: Macmillan

Gore, John (ed) 1985 *Thomas Creevey's Papers*. Harmondsworth: Penguin

Hardwick, Michael 1973 *A Literary Atlas and Gazetteer of the British Isles*. Newton Abbott: David and Charles

Holmes, Richard 2003 *Wellington: The Iron Duke*. London: HarperCollins

Hudson, W H 1982 *Afoot in England*. Oxford: Oxford University Press

Kilvert, Robert Francis (a selection chosen, edited and introduced by William Plomer) 1999 *Kilvert's Diary*. London: Pimlico

Lockhart, J G (with an introduction by W M Parker) 1969 *The Life of Sir Walter Scott*. London: Dent

Tomalin, Claire 2002 *Samuel Pepys: The Unequalled Self*. London: Viking

Walpole, Horace (with an introduction and notes by P W Hammond) 1987 *Historic Doubts on the Life and Reign of Richard the Third*. Gloucester: Sutton

Wilson, Angus 1994 *The Strange Ride of Rudyard Kipling: His Life and Work*. London: Pimlico

Winstone, H V F 1993 *Gertrude Bell*. London: Constable